RIVER COTTAGE

GREAT
PIES

PASTIES, PUDS AND MORE

RIVER COTTAGE
GREAT
PIES

GELF ALDERSON

Hugh Fearnley-Whittingstall's
RIVER COTTAGE

BLOOMSBURY PUBLISHING
LONDON · OXFORD · NEW YORK · NEW DELHI · SYDNEY

To Hayley, who means everything to me and loves a pie!

Recipe notes

- All spoon measures are level unless otherwise stated:
  1 tsp = 5ml spoon; 1 tbsp = 15ml spoon.
- All herbs are fresh unless otherwise suggested.
- Use freshly ground or cracked black pepper unless otherwise listed.
- All veg and fruit should be washed. Choose organic fruit and veg if possible.
- Root veg, onions, garlic and ginger are peeled or scrubbed unless otherwise suggested.
- If using the zest of citrus fruit, choose unwaxed fruit.
- Please use free-range eggs, preferably organic.
- Opt for organic products where possible, including tinned pulses, yoghurt and cheeses.
- Oven timings are provided for both conventional and fan-assisted ovens. Individual ovens can deviate by 10°C or more either way from the actual setting, so get to know your oven and use an oven thermometer to check the temperature.

Contents

Foreword

I've always had a deep affection for pies. There are recipes for them in all my books, whether pastry-topped, filo-wrapped or bubbling away under a layer of mash. I think the perpetual appeal of pies (apart from the sheer deliciousness of a good crust) is that they are resolutely traditional, while also being modernise-able. You can put pretty much anything in a pie or tart and they are satisfying to cook. They may require a little work to put together but there is nothing to beat the moment when they emerge, resplendent and steaming from the oven, needing only simply cooked veg or a jug of custard on the side – if that. They are the very apex of comfort cooking.

Gelf Alderson has worked with us at River Cottage for over a decade now. He has shaped the River Cottage kitchen and repertoire as much as it has shaped him, and that wonderful symbiosis is evident in these pages. He treats us to familiar recipes – spanakopita, chicken and mushroom pie and a classic stargazy with its heavenward-looking sardines. He's shared inventive recipes too. There's a dhal pie, a merguez-spiced squash and dried apricot pie, a pie with a spicy meatball and olive filling and a fennel-dusted pastry. And you'll find a plum, raspberry and hazelnut meringue pie and a treacle toffee pear strudel in the lovely sweet chapter.

True to the River Cottage ethos, the chapter on vegetable pies is right up at the front – and there are lots of vegetarian-friendly recipes scattered throughout the other chapters too, all liberally seasoned with delicious combinations of herbs, spices and aromatics. There's plenty of meat and fish as well – but always generously supported with veg (and/or fruit), showing the power of plants to deliver flavour, balance and virtue in a well-rounded pie!

One of the things that makes this book stand out is its dismantling of the mystique that surrounds pastry-making. Yes, you do have to follow a few rules, but it's entirely achievable by pretty much anyone. I've heard the rumour that only people with naturally cold hands can make good pastry, or that it's a knack you either have or you don't. I think it's all nonsense! The only magic ingredient is confidence, and Gelf will give you that in spades. Aided by excellent step-by-step photography, he devotes an entire chapter to this essential pie building-block, and demonstrates just how straightforward pastry-making actually is. There's even a simple method for filo, which brilliantly de-mystifies this most enigmatic and tempting of pastries. And Gelf rightly encourages us to get a bit more goodness into our pastries by sometimes incorporating wholegrain flours too.

I'm proud of all the titles that have cantered out of the River Cottage stable over the years, but I have to say this one looks particularly hard to resist. Emma Lee's superb photography captures the spirit of our food – generous and beautiful, but in a totally relaxed kind of way. Above all, though, *River Cottage Great Pies* is a mouth-watering read and a highly pragmatic guide, created by a true foodie. Gelf's passion comes through on every page, and makes this book the lovely, celebratory thing it is. Just like a great pie.

Hugh

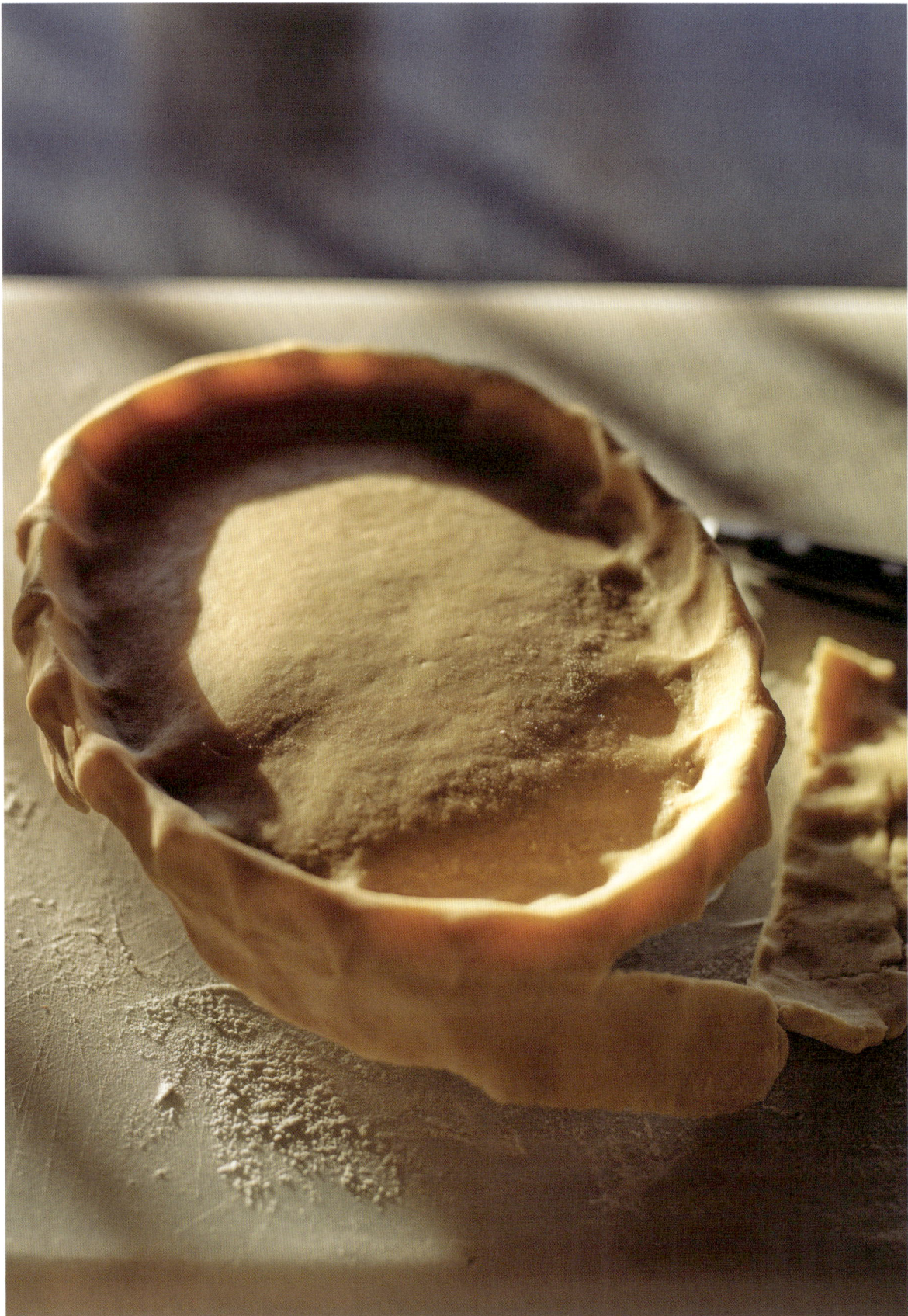

Introduction

Pies are so ingrained in our national identity that everyone I talk to about them instantly reels off their favourites with glee. And it's no wonder, pies have been made in some form or other for centuries – not just here in the UK but all over the world. They're lauded in paintings, tapestries, ancient songs and familiar nursery rhymes. Often depicted gracing the highest table in the lands, pies were the centrepiece of many a royal banquet and celebration. Equally, they've been filled with the humblest of ingredients for everyday meals since bygone days. I'd say pies have not just stood the test of time, they have conquered it!

Diversifying into a multitude of forms and infiltrating all of our food lives, pies are here to stay, which is why I've written this book to celebrate them. I have filled the pages with both River Cottage classics and my own favourite pies, all of which are not only absolutely delicious but also super-achievable!

One potential hurdle with pies is the key ingredient, which comes with something of a tricky reputation, and that's the pastry. This is why I've dedicated the first chapter to upping your pastry game. Here you'll find my recipes for the classic pastries that I have been perfecting in the kitchen for over 25 years. To make these as reliable as possible every time, for several of the pastries I've given an exact weight for beaten egg, rather than stipulating the number of eggs. This also makes the recipes easy to scale down as well as up, and you don't need to worry about wastage – any leftover egg will be used for egg wash.

You may find my shortcrust and sweet pasties (on pages 16 and 20) are a bit stickier than you're used to, but have faith and don't be tempted to throw more flour in! Once rested and chilled, they will be easy to roll out and you'll be able to move the pastry around easily as you roll. So lining tart cases becomes a breeze! You'll also probably notice that my method for lining pastry cases and baking them 'blind' (without the filling) on page 27 is different from your average recipe. The initial cook is a lot longer and there are a fair few steps, but stick with it to get that perfect crisp pastry every time.

The individual pastry recipes use different flours and it is important to adhere to the type of flour specified. For example, you need softer, lower-in-protein plain flour for shortcrust pastry, but stronger bread flour for rough puff. I've included wholemeal alternatives for some of the pastries – you'll find including wholemeal flour gives the flavour a real boost, as well as being better for you. Note that you will need more water if using wholemeal flour, as it's a lot more thirsty.

A lot of the pies and tarts throughout the book can be made with whatever pastry takes your fancy, so don't get too hung up on using shortcrust or rough puff. This applies particularly to the recipes in Veggie Pies (pages 49–73) and Saucy Pies (pages 105–131). You'll work out your favourite, as I have over the years. If you haven't got time to make rough puff you can always knock up a quick shortcrust instead. I'd always encourage you to make your own pastry but you can buy ready-made good-quality filo and all-butter puff pastry if you're really pressed for time. That said, I'm confident that my recipes will set you on a relatively stress-free pastry adventure, which will be mouth-watering and fun in equal amounts!

Whether you're looking for a comforting dinner, something to fill a picnic basket, or a sculptured raised pie, you'll find something appealing in this book. If you love a quiche, try my recipe (on page 76). It's with no shame that I call it 'the ultimate quiche'! Buttery, biscuity shortcrust pastry encases a sumptuous filling of sweet caramelised onions in a creamy custard richly flavoured with cheese and parsley. It's a recipe that will confine inferior shop-bought imitations to history.

Having made the West Country my home, I felt it was only right to dedicate a short chapter to the mighty pasty. The true home of the pasty is still hotly contested, but I'd rather focus on how delicious they. Pasties are, of course, popular nationwide, but you can also find versions of them all around the world. Originally created for eating on the go, these pastry superstars are perfect for picnics and lunch boxes, but they are more often served up for dinner in my house.

Beyond traditional pies and pasties, I've delved into the world of tarts and steamed puddings. And, of course, I've devoted a lengthy chapter to sweet stuff. Desserts have always been close to my heart (and mouth), as I spent a few years as a pastry chef early on in my career. In the sweet chapter on pages 189–225 you'll find my favourite classics as well as some more funky recipes bursting with fruit. I've also given you my well-honed vanilla custard tart (page 201), irresistible salted caramel glazed éclairs (page 220) and a couple of indulgent tarts for chocolate lovers. Here you'll find everything you need to wow people around the dinner table.

You will need some kit for the recipes in this book, but not a lot. Invest in a good rolling pin and pastry brush, plus a pie dish or two, a few tart tins, a couple of roasting trays and sturdy baking trays and you're good to go. I've given the dimensions of the dishes I've used for the pies and tarts but don't be restricted by these. It's unlikely that your cupboards will be filled with identical dishes to mine and there's no need to run out and buy a whole load more. If your dish is wider and shallower, you may need a touch more pastry and slightly shorter cooking time; the opposite applies if your dish is narrower and deeper.

Most ovenproof dishes are suitable for cooking pies. Ovenproof pans work particularly well – I have a few cast-iron skillets which are not only versatile, but they look great and will last forever. So, if you are looking to splash out on some new pans I'd highly recommend buying a couple of these in different sizes – you'll find yourself using them all the time.

The one thing I think is an absolute must is at least a couple of good-quality loose-bottomed metal tart tins, of different sizes. Metal conducts heat far better than ceramic, so your pastry will cook better in these tins. Also, being able to lift the tart out easily on the metal base while it is still hot will allow any steam to escape, so the pastry doesn't sweat. Just being able to see that sharp pastry crust emerge is so enticing!

So, let's dust off that apron, get our rolling pins ready and start to enjoy pastry-making. We know pastry tastes good but it is so much more wonderful when you make it yourself and eat it when it's truly fresh and crisp. It still thrills me to this day and I'm excited to share all of this with you.

1
PASTRIES & TECHNIQUES

This is where it all starts. Getting the pastry just right is key to making fabulous pies and tarts, not least because well-made pastry is easy to work with. Here I'm focusing on the familiar pastries I use in this book, giving you an understanding of the basic ingredients and techniques. Follow the straightforward methods I've been honing over the years and you'll be making pastry like a pro in no time.

Once you've mastered the basic pastry recipes, you'll have the confidence to prepare any of the recipes in the chapters that follow. And on your journey to pastry perfection, from shortcrust to rough puff, you'll be able to adapt existing recipes and create new ones with whatever pastry you decide to use.

With some of the pastry recipes, I give a weight of beaten egg to ensure your proportion of liquid to flour is super-accurate and your pastry has the right consistency. So, you are likely to have a little egg left over, but that just means you don't have to crack another egg for your egg wash, which can be wasteful. And talking of waste, don't discard any leftover pastry – turn it into little jam tarts or apple turnovers, which I enjoyed so much as a kid!

Pastry has a reputation for being difficult but it's important not to be intimidated by it. With the techniques I use, everything in this chapter is achievable and not too faffy. I've taken the stress out of pastry-making, so you can enjoy the eating!

Shortcrust pastry

This is the most versatile of all pastries. Whether you're looking for a short, biscuity case for a tart or a soft pastry topping for a pie, shortcrust is the one. If you've made it before and been disappointed by the result, give my fail-safe recipe a go. It is perfect for all savoury pies, pasties, tarts and flans. For meat pies and pasties you can substitute half the butter with lard.

To ensure a consistent result, I give a weight of egg. It's also important to use plain white or fine wholemeal flour (not strong bread flour). If the flour is stoneground, you may need extra egg as it tends to be more thirsty. Be sure to use fridge-cold butter and keep everything nice and cold.

Work the mix only enough to bring it together. The pastry can feel sticky, especially in a warm kitchen (or if you have warm hands!) but don't be tempted to throw on more flour. Instead, use a dough scraper to move it around. Flatten the pastry and shape it into a disc before resting – you'll find it much easier than a chilled ball of pastry to roll out thinly. It will also stay cold and be easier to move around and work with. And you'll only need a little flour for rolling it out because cold pastry doesn't really stick.

Makes about 500g

260g plain flour, or 130g each
   plain and fine wholemeal flour
A pinch of salt
130g cold butter, diced
130g beaten egg
   (about 2¼ medium eggs)

Put the flour and salt into a large bowl, add the butter (1) and rub together using your fingers (2) or palms of your hands until a fine breadcrumb texture is achieved (3). Don't continue to work the pastry past this point. (You can use a food processor to speed up this stage, pulsing to avoid overworking, then transfer the mix to a bowl.)

Add the beaten egg (4) and mix quickly using your hands, to combine and bring the dough together.

Turn out onto an unfloured surface and knead briefly (5) for no more than a minute until the dough is smooth. Avoid overworking, as it will result in a tough pastry. Flatten the pastry into a disc, wrap tightly in baking paper (6) and place in the fridge to rest for an hour.

Unwrap the pastry and knead briefly on an unfloured surface. Lightly dust a work surface and your rolling pin with flour and roll the pastry out to your required thickness (7). Then roll it around the rolling pin (8) to make it easier to lift over your pie dish or tart tin.

technique illustrated overleaf

Sweet pastry

This is a sweet version of shortcrust, so the same rules apply. Weigh your beaten egg, keep everything cold and don't overwork it. The pastry will be sticky when you make it, so use a dough scraper (as you would for bread) to gather the dough. Once rested and chilled, you can roll this pastry with almost no flour until it is thin enough to see through and, as long as it stays cold, you can pick it up and move it around with ease. This means you can get that thin, sharp pastry you see with tarts coming out of a professional kitchen.

Makes about 500g

240g plain flour
65g icing sugar, sifted
A pinch of salt
120g cold butter, diced
75g beaten egg (about
  1¼ medium eggs)

Put the flour, icing sugar and salt into a large bowl, add the diced butter and rub together using your fingers (1) or palms of your hands until a fine breadcrumb texture is achieved. Be careful not to continue to work the pastry past this point as it could lead to a doughy pastry. (Alternatively, you could use a food processor to speed up this stage, pulsing the mix to avoid overworking, then transfer it to a bowl.)

Add the beaten egg (2) and mix quickly using your hands (3) to combine and bring the dough together.

Turn out onto an unfloured work surface (4) and knead quickly for no more than a minute. The dough should feel a little sticky but smooth – a bit like fudge (5). Avoid overworking, as it will result in a tough pastry.

Flatten the pastry into a disc (6), wrap tightly in baking paper and place in the fridge to rest for an hour.

After resting, remove the pastry from the fridge, unwrap and knead briefly on an unfloured surface.

Lightly flour a work surface and your rolling pin and roll the pastry out (7) to your required thickness, usually 3mm (though I was trained to a maximum of 2mm for sweet pastry!). If you lift the pastry up, you should be able to see through it (8).

technique illustrated overleaf

To line a tart tin with shortcrust or sweet pastry and 'bake blind'

You may notice a few key differences in the way I prepare a pastry case compared to other recipes. Firstly, I like to blind bake the case (i.e. filled with baking beans) for longer at a lower temperature. This enables the pastry to cook fully before you remove the beans, without gaining too much colour. So, when it comes to the final bake, the pastry doesn't burn.

I always return the pastry case to the oven once the beans are removed to complete the cooking process and crisp up the base. And I consider the final process of sealing the pastry with egg wash vital to stop any liquid filling from soaking into the pastry and making it soggy. After all the work you've done to get it biscuity, you really want to avoid this!

I'd also recommend giving the peeler trick a go instead of using a knife to trim the pastry – it's revolutionary.

Preheat the oven to 180°C/160°C Fan/Gas 4.

Grease your tart tin with softened butter, using an odd bit of baking paper (or butter wrapping) and then dust with flour, knocking the flour into every corner and then knocking out any excess.

Roll out the pastry on a lightly floured work surface to your desired thickness (usually 3mm) and about 5cm larger than the diameter of your tart tin, rotating the pastry occasionally. Roll the pastry around the pin so you can pick it up easily and transfer it to the tart tin (1).

Unroll the pastry over the top of the tart tin (2), lifting the outside of the pastry at the same time (to relieve any pressure), carefully using a knuckle rather than a fingertip. Push the pastry into the corners of the tart tin (3). Continue around the base of the tin.

Break off a little pastry from the overhang and form into a ball. Dip this dobber (as I call it) in flour and use to push the pastry into the corners (4); you're less likely to break the pastry than if you use your fingers. Trim away the excess, leaving a 2cm overhang; keep the trim for repairs.

continued overleaf

Prick the pastry base all over with a fork to allow steam to escape. I also pierce the sides in a few places (5). Place the tart tin on a baking tray.

Line the pastry case with baking paper (6) and fill to the brim with baking beans (7).

Transfer to the oven and bake blind for 35–40 minutes. Remove from the oven and carefully lift out the paper full of beans. (Leave the beans to cool and keep them for your next bake.)

Carefully trim the pastry edge using a serrated knife, or gradually shave it with a vegetable peeler until flush with the top of the tart tin, cutting away from the case and using your other hand to stabilise the pastry. (If you push the knife towards the case, it will snap the crust inwards.) If you have any cracks, push a bit of the raw pastry into each crack, smoothing it in to seal. Discard the rest of the pastry trim.

Return the tart case to the oven for a further 10 minutes, or until it is dry and there is no sign of any raw-looking grey pastry.

To make an egg wash, beat an egg to combine (or a few egg yolks together for a super seal) and brush all around the inside of the case while the pastry is still hot (8). This will seal any fork holes and stop any filling escaping.

Return the tart case to the oven for a couple of minutes to cook the egg wash and seal the pastry. Your tart case is now ready to go.

Rough puff pastry

Life is too short to make classic puff pastry and I prefer rough puff anyway, as it doesn't go so flaky that it loses all its substance. The real key to getting a good rise is to keep the pastry cold. This can make it a little hard to roll between folds, but the result is worth it. To start with the pastry may feel dry and tough to work with, but after it's rested the first time it will be easier to work with. Rough puff freezes well, so you may want to double up the quantities and keep a batch in the freezer.

Makes about 1kg

500g strong white bread flour
   (or 375g strong white and
   125g fine wholemeal)
A large pinch of salt
250g cold butter, diced
About 250ml ice-cold water

Mix the flour and salt together in a large bowl. Add the butter (1) and toss to coat the pieces in the flour (2). Add enough ice-cold water (3) to bring the mixture together and form a dough; the butter should still be in small cubes, not mixed into the flour.

Turn the dough out onto a well-floured surface and flour your rolling pin. Roll out the dough (4) to a rectangle, 5mm thick, repeatedly lifting and turning the pastry, and re-flouring the rolling pin as well as underneath and on top of the pastry to prevent sticking. You should see big smears of butter running through the pastry (5).

Fold one third of the pastry into the middle and the other third over the top (6). Turn the pastry 90° and roll out to a rectangle again, then repeat the folding. Wrap tightly in baking paper and rest in the fridge for 45 minutes.

Remove the pastry from the fridge and unwrap it. Roll into a rectangle, fold and rest in the fridge as before (7); you should still have streaks of butter running through the pastry.

Repeat this process of refrigerating, rolling and folding at least twice more, giving a total of 4 roll and folds, but ideally until the streaks of butter have disappeared (8).

After the fourth roll, fold and chill, remove the pastry from the fridge, lightly flour a work surface and your rolling pin and roll out the pastry to your required thickness.

technique illustrated overleaf

Hot water crust pastry

This turns all the pastry rules on their head, as you use hot (rather than chilled) fats. The technique of mixing hot melted fat into the flour makes the pastry incredibly strong and heat resistant, so you can bake whatever you fill it with for a long time without risk of the pastry burning. It also happens to be delicious! This dough is really sticky when you make it, but don't panic and add lots of extra flour. Just wrap it up and rest it in the fridge, as instructed, for at least 4 hours. When you take it out, it will be a beautiful fudgy consistency and a joy to work with.

Makes about 1kg

100g butter
100g lard (or use an extra 100g
   butter for a vegetarian option)
200ml water
550g plain flour (or 450g plain
   and 100g fine wholemeal)
A large pinch of salt

Put the butter, lard and water into a saucepan and heat gently until the fats have melted (1); do not allow to boil as this will reduce the volume of liquid and lead to a dry, cracking pastry. Allow to cool slightly, until you can comfortably put your finger in it.

Place the flour and salt in a bowl, add the hot liquid (2) and quickly mix together using a wooden spoon to form a dough.

Turn the dough out onto a work surface and knead quickly until smooth (3).

Form the dough into a disc or rectangle, wrap tightly in baking paper (4) and place in the fridge to rest for a minimum of 4 hours, preferably overnight.

Lightly flour a work surface and your rolling pin and roll the pastry out to your required thickness.

To fill a raised pie

A raised pie is a magnificent centrepiece and can be the star of the show. For a classic round raised pie, I use a loose-bottomed springform cake tin. For a Gala pie or pâté en croûte, I use a terrine or loaf tin. Unlike the previous pastries, it isn't wise to roll hot water crust too thin as it will crack and all that lovely jelly will run out and be lost! If this is your first attempt, don't get too hung up on perfecting the crimping – just make sure the edges are properly sealed.

To assemble the pie, cut off a generous quarter of the pastry and set aside; this will be your lid.

On a lightly floured surface, roll out the bigger piece of pastry to a 1cm thick, large round or rectangle, depending on whether you are making a round pie in a springform cake tin or an oblong pie in a terrine or loaf tin. (If you are using a 20cm cake tin, the pastry needs to be around 35cm in diameter.)

Lift the pastry round on the rolling pin and drape it over your tin. Press the pastry onto the base and sides to line the tin and overlap the sides by at least 1cm (1).

Roll out the reserved portion of pastry for the lid to a round (the diameter of your tin), or to a rectangle (the dimensions of your tin or terrine), and about 1cm thick.

Spoon your chosen filling into the pastry case, filling it to the brim (2) and pressing it down evenly. Trim the pastry roughly, leaving a little overhang.

Brush the edges of the lining pastry with a little egg wash and lay the pastry lid on top of the pie. Press the edges together to seal and trim away the excess pastry (3).

Crimp the pastry edge by pinching between thumb and finger to form peaks, or use a rounded knife blade to push down towards the edge of the tin in evenly spaced indentations (4).

Filo pastry

This pastry is so bafflingly thin and delicate, most people wouldn't consider making it, opting for ready-made filo instead. The traditional method calls for filo to be skilfully stretched and pulled, but this recipe is more straightforward and yields good results. The key is to roll it super-thin on a surface dusted with plenty of cornflour – to get that beautiful shard-like crispness on baking. You'll need to keep it from being exposed to the air for long otherwise it will dry out and become unusable.

Makes about 500g

350g plain flour
6g fine salt
30ml olive oil
170ml water, heated to 50°C
Cornflour, to dust

Put the flour, salt, olive oil and water into a large bowl (1) and mix with your hands to combine (2) and form a rough dough. Transfer it to a work surface.

Work the dough vigorously for 3–4 minutes (3) until it is smooth and soft. Form into a long cylinder (4) and cut into 12 equal pieces (5), each about 60g.

Dust a large baking sheet with cornflour. Roll the filo pieces into balls (6) and place on the baking sheet. Cover with a damp tea towel and leave to rest at room temperature for at least an hour.

Lightly dust your rolling pin and surface with cornflour. Giving yourself plenty of space, roll out a filo pastry ball thinly (7), continually turning and dusting underneath with more cornflour. You're aiming for a 0.5mm thickness so keep going, trying to keep your rolling nice and even!

Once the fine thickness is achieved, immediately lift the pastry sheet (8) onto a baking sheet lightly dusted with cornflour and cover with a lightly dampened cloth.

Repeat to roll out the next ball of filo dough. Once the thickness is achieved, remove the cloth from the first sheet of pastry, lightly dust that sheet with cornflour and place the second filo sheet directly on top. Re-cover with the damp cloth and repeat this process until all the balls are rolled out. You will need to use the pastry straight away or keep dampening the cloth to stop it drying out.

technique illustrated overleaf

5

6

7

8

Suet pastry

This is a classic British pastry used for traditional steamed puddings –
both sweet and savoury – and dumplings. It is the easiest of pastries, as
you mix it and use it straight away. I think it's particularly delicious made
with self-raising wholemeal flour and freshly minced beef suet, which
lends flavour unlike the shop-bought alternative – you should be able
to get this from your butcher.

Makes about 1kg

480g self-raising flour
    (or wholemeal self-raising flour)
240g suet or frozen butter, grated
A large pinch of salt
360ml water

Place the flour, suet or grated butter and salt in a large
bowl (1) and toss together. Add the water (2) and mix
quickly with your hands to form a soft dough.

Turn out onto a lightly floured surface and knead for
1 minute (3). Use straight away (4) as the raising agent
will now be active and will only keep working well for
a relatively short period of time.

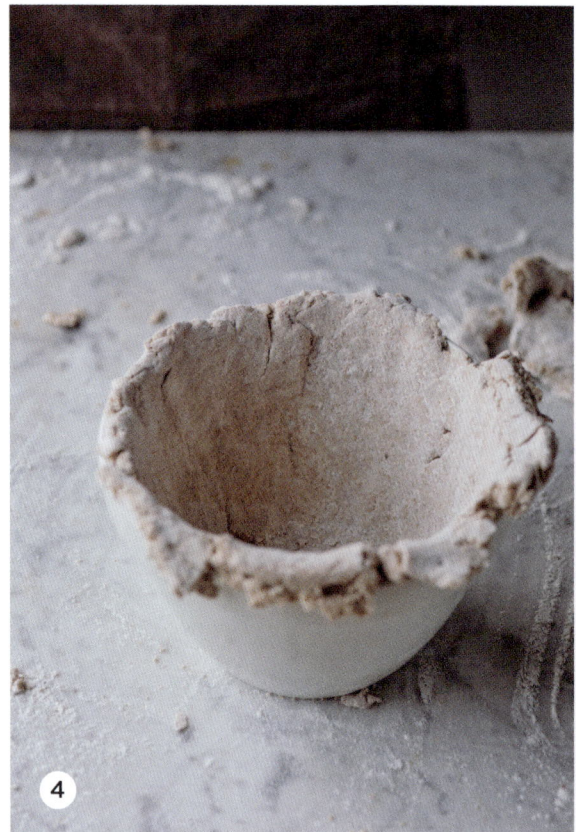

To line a pudding basin with suet pastry

Grease your pudding basin with softened butter, using an odd end of baking paper, and then dust with flour, knocking out any excess. Split off one-third of your pastry and keep to one side.

On a lightly floured surface, roll out the larger piece of pastry to a round, just under 1cm thick. Gather the sides of the pastry and drop the middle into the base of the pudding basin (1).

Push the pastry gently onto the bottom of the basin and smooth it around the sides, leaving a good 2cm overhanging the top. As you line the sides, the pastry will naturally form a thick crease. Working from the bottom of the crease, push the pastry to the side of the basin and up towards the top (2), so the overlapping pastry becomes the same thickness as the rest and the excess is squeezed up and out of the basin (3). Trim the overhang to 2cm all the way around (4).

Spoon your chosen filling into the pastry-lined pudding basin, leaving at least 2cm clear at the top of the basin. Brush the top of the pastry rim with egg wash or water.

On your lightly floured surface, roll out the other one-third of the pastry to a round, just under 1cm thick. Lay this over top of the basin and then pinch the top of the lining pastry and the lid together to form a tightly sealed crust. Don't worry too much how this looks as it will be the bottom of the pudding once it is tipped out!

Choux pastry

This pastry has a reputation for being difficult to master, but if you follow the key stages detailed in my method, you'll realise it's one of the quickest and easiest pastries to make. If you shape your choux into little buns, bake and cool them, all you need is some whipped cream and chocolate sauce to have dessert on the table in under an hour! It's your go-to pastry for choux buns (sweet and savoury) and éclairs, as well as profiteroles.

Makes enough for 4 large éclairs
or 20 small choux buns

50g butter
150ml water
60g strong white bread flour, sifted
A pinch of salt
1 tsp sugar (optional)
130g beaten egg
   (about 2¼ medium eggs)

Preheat the oven to 220°C/210°C Fan/Gas 7.

Put the butter and water into a saucepan (1) and place over a medium heat until the butter is melted. Turn up the heat and bring to the boil.

As soon as the liquid boils, add the flour, salt and sugar, if using, and mix with a wooden spoon. Turn the heat down and beat the mixture vigorously over the heat with the spoon; this is one of the crucial stages. Keep beating until the mixture comes away from the sides of the pan (2).

The mixture will start to become shiny; this is the fat starting to almost split out. If you pinch the mixture (careful, it's hot!), it should leave a film of grease on your fingers and not stick to them (3).

Tip the mixture into a large bowl, swap your wooden spoon for a whisk and whisk the mixture for a minute to release some of the heat (4). (It should be cooled to about 50°C before you add the eggs.)

Add half of the beaten egg and whisk vigorously until combined (5); don't panic if it starts to split – just keep whisking hard and it will come together.

Add the remaining beaten egg, gradually (6), beating well after each addition to make a shiny, soft paste (7), thick enough to be piped or spooned (8). Use and bake immediately (to make choux buns, as described on page 223, or éclairs, page 220).

technique illustrated overleaf

2
VEGGIE PIES

Pies have a meaty history, but here at River Cottage we love our veg and, with my vegetarian background, a pie filled with a bounty of vegetables has been the cornerstone of many a supper over the years. And why not? The variety the veg world offers us is so much greater than meat provides, with hundreds of different textures, colours and flavours to choose from. I never get bored of cooking with veg, as you'll see here. Hopefully, you'll find a few new ideas to keep you excited about veg, or maybe give you the tools to convert someone still not convinced of their magnificence.

I love to spice up veg and there's plenty of that happening in this chapter, from the Curried potato, spinach and paneer pie on page 59 to the Merguez spiced squash and apricot pie on page 68. Spice just goes so well with buttery, crispy pastry; the pairing is irresistible every time. There are also lots of classic flavour combinations used in interesting ways, like my Cauliflower cheese filo pie (page 65) and Tomato, beetroot and tarragon steamed pudding (page 56), so if you fancy a spicy supper or a cosy comfort dinner this is the chapter for you.

We all know eating more veg is key for our health, so source some seasonal veg, make your favourite pastry and get one of these pies in the oven. I guarantee you'll find some new favourites here... I know my staunchly vegetarian family will!

Spanakopita

I've been lucky enough to visit Greece many times and this is my favourite thing to pick up for breakfast. You can almost always find a great local bakery selling warm slabs of spanakopita wherever you go. I've added a handful of pumpkin seeds and some herbs for a little crunch and aroma; hopefully this won't upset purists too much!

Serves 4

5 filo pastry sheets, about
    300g in total (page 37)
Olive oil, to brush

For the filling
300g spinach (tougher stalks
    removed and roughly chopped
    if using large leaf spinach)
200g feta
50g pumpkin seeds, toasted
A small bunch of basil or oregano,
    leaves picked and roughly
    chopped
2 medium eggs, beaten
Sea salt and freshly cracked
    black pepper

Preheat the oven to 200°C/180°C Fan/Gas 6. Generously brush a 22cm round (or 20cm square) loose-bottomed cake tin with olive oil.

For the filling, place a large saucepan over a medium heat and add the spinach (with just the water clinging to the leaves after washing). Pop on a lid and stir every 30 seconds until the spinach is wilted down. Tip it into a sieve to drain and cool slightly, then place in the centre of a clean cloth. Wrap the cloth around the spinach and give it a good squeeze to remove excess moisture.

Crumble the feta into a large bowl. Add the spinach, toasted pumpkin seeds, chopped basil or oregano and beaten eggs. Mix together well, seasoning with salt and pepper, but go easy on the salt as feta is quite salty.

Drape a sheet of filo into the oiled cake tin to line the base and sides, allowing it to overhang the rim of the tin and brush the pastry with olive oil. Layer another 3 filo sheets in the tin, slightly off-centre so you have plenty of overhang to cover the top, brushing each with oil.

Spoon in the spinach and feta filling and cover with the remaining filo sheet. Fold the overhanging pastry over the top. It's nice not to be too neat, as scrunchy bits will crisp up in the oven to delicious effect.

Brush the top with olive oil and bake in the oven for 30–35 minutes until the pastry is lovely and golden. Cut into wedges and serve warm or at room temperature.

Creamy field mushroom, celeriac and leek pie

I love celeriac and it loves being cooked with mushrooms and blue cheese. After a long woodland walk this is a perfect autumn supper, especially if I've been lucky (and brave enough) to pick some wild mushrooms and thrown them in too. Remember, only cook with wine you like to drink, mainly so you can enjoy a glass while you're waiting for the pie to bake.

Serves 4–6

500g rough puff (page 28) or
   shortcrust pastry (page 16)
Flour, to dust
Egg wash (beaten egg)

For the filling
1kg celeriac, peeled and cut into
   1cm cubes
10 shallots (or 3 small onions,
   quartered)
4 tbsp extra virgin olive oil
1kg large flat mushrooms,
   quartered
2 leeks, trimmed and finely
   chopped
4 garlic cloves, finely chopped
3 sprigs of thyme
250ml full-bodied red wine
2 tbsp soy sauce
300ml double cream
150g rich blue cheese, such as
   Devon Blue, crumbled
Sea salt and freshly cracked
   black pepper

Preheat the oven to 200°C/180°C Fan/Gas 6.

For the filling, put the celeriac and shallots (or onions) into a shallow roasting tray, trickle over half the olive oil, season with salt and pepper and tumble together. Cook in the oven for 10 minutes, then take out the tray, add the mushrooms and give everything a stir. Return to the oven for 15–20 minutes until the veg are just starting to soften.

Meanwhile, place a medium saucepan over a medium-low heat and add the remaining olive oil. Toss in the leeks with the garlic and thyme and sweat for 8–10 minutes until soft.

Turn the heat up to high and add the wine and soy sauce. Let it bubble rapidly until reduced by half. Add the cream and crumbled blue cheese and bring to a simmer, stirring. Cook, stirring, until the sauce is thickened.

Take the tray from the oven. Tip the veg into the creamy leek sauce, picking out any thyme stalks, then taste and season accordingly. Transfer to a pie dish or roasting pan, about 25cm in diameter and 5cm deep. Leave to cool.

Roll out the pastry on a lightly floured surface to a round, no thinner than 5mm and slightly bigger than your pie dish. Drape the pastry over the filling and press the edges onto the rim of the dish or pan. Trim away the excess and crimp the edges.

Brush the pastry lid with egg wash and pierce in a couple of places. Bake in the oven for 30 minutes until the pastry is risen and golden brown. Serve hot from the oven.

Jerusalem artichoke, shallot, chestnut and kale pie

Jerusalem artichokes are one of my favourite autumnal veg. They may be a faff to prepare but it's well worth it for their earthy, rich flavour, which pairs well with kale and chestnuts. As we like to say, 'What grows together goes together', and as the chestnuts are falling from the trees the first artichokes are ready to pull. Select a nice dry cider for this one and sample it through the cooking process.

Serves 4-6

300g rough puff (page 28) or
   shortcrust pastry (page 16)
Flour, to dust
Egg wash (beaten egg)

For the filling
500g shallots, halved
1kg Jerusalem artichokes, peeled
   and cut into 2cm pieces
3 garlic cloves, finely sliced
3 tbsp extra virgin olive oil
150g cooked chestnuts, chopped
100ml dry cider
300ml double cream
5 sprigs of thyme
100g kale, tough stalks removed,
   shredded
Sea salt and freshly cracked
   black pepper

Preheat the oven to 200°C/180°C Fan/Gas 6.

For the filling, put the shallots, artichokes, garlic and olive oil into a roasting tray, season with salt and pepper and tumble together. Roast in the oven for 25–30 minutes until the artichokes are starting to soften, then add the chestnuts and cook for a further 5 minutes.

Meanwhile, put the cider, cream and thyme into a large saucepan and bring to the boil over a high heat. Let it bubble until the cream reduces and starts to thicken, then lower the heat and pick out the thyme.

Add the kale to the cream and cook until it wilts, then add the roasted artichoke and chestnut mix. Stir gently, then taste and season accordingly. Tip the filling into a pie dish, about 25cm in diameter and 5cm deep. Leave to cool down.

Roll out the pastry on a lightly floured surface until slightly larger all round than your dish and no thinner than 5mm. Drape the pastry over the pie dish and press the edges onto the rim of the dish. Trim away the excess and crimp the edges.

Brush the pie lid with egg wash, pierce in a few places and cook in the oven for 25–30 minutes until the pastry is golden brown. Serve hot from the oven.

Tomato, beetroot and tarragon steamed pudding

Steak and kidney isn't the only savoury steamed pud! This veg filling is so vibrant it's a real treat when you cut into the pudding and it tumbles out. And it's not just good-looking – caraway, cumin and fresh chilli pack in a punch of flavour as well. Try to get lovely small beetroots in a bunch.

Serves 4–6

For the filling
250g beetroot
3 tbsp cold-pressed rapeseed oil
1 onion, finely sliced
2 garlic cloves, finely sliced
½ medium-heat red chilli, halved, deseeded and finely sliced
1 tsp caraway seeds
1 tsp ground cumin
400g tin chopped tomatoes
250g cherry vine tomatoes
A small bunch of tarragon, leaves picked and finely chopped
Sea salt and freshly cracked black pepper

For the pastry
1kg freshly made suet pastry (page 40)
Butter, to grease
Flour, to dust
Egg wash (beaten egg; optional)

First make the filling. Put the beetroot into a medium saucepan, cover with water and bring to the boil. Lower the heat and simmer for 35–40 minutes until tender (a knife inserted in the centre should pass through easily). Drain and leave until cool enough to handle, then rub the skins off and cut the beetroot into 2cm pieces.

While the beets are cooking, heat the oil in a pan over a low heat. Add the onion, garlic and chilli and cook slowly until the onion is softened. Sprinkle in the spices and stir for a minute, then add the tinned tomatoes. Simmer for 15–20 minutes, stirring often, until starting to thicken.

Add the beetroot, cherry tomatoes and tarragon, and cook for a couple of minutes until the tomato skins just start to split. Taste and season accordingly. Remove from the heat.

Grease and flour a 1 litre pudding basin. Following the instructions on page 43, line the basin with two-thirds of the suet pastry. Spoon in the filling, cover with the remaining pastry and seal the pastry edges.

Cover the basin with a pleated sheet of foil, securing it with string under the rim. Stand the basin on a small plate or trivet in a large, deep pan and pour in enough boiling water to come halfway up its sides. Put the lid on the pan and bring to a simmer over a medium heat. Steam the pud for 45 minutes, topping up the boiling water as necessary.

Lift out the basin and remove the foil. Loosen the sides of the pudding with the tip of a knife, then invert onto a warmed plate. Serve at once, with greens.

Curried potato, spinach and paneer pie

Paneer is a simple and quick cheese to make and you can use it instead
of halloumi in almost all recipes. Here, I've added it to a lovely potato and
spinach curry, and the salty, creamy cheese really complements the spices.
I think you'll find it will become a favourite curry pretty quickly. I'm a bit
of a chilli wimp so I keep my curries quite mild but if you like yours hot
feel free to add as many chillies as you can take!

Serves 4

500g shortcrust pastry (page 16)
Flour, to dust
Egg wash (beaten egg)

For the paneer
2 litres whole milk
Juice of 1 lemon (approximately)
1 tsp salt

For the filling
4 tbsp light rapeseed oil
2 onions, finely sliced
50g fresh ginger, finely grated
6 garlic cloves, finely chopped
2 tsp ground cumin
1 tsp ground coriander
1 tsp ground turmeric
1 tsp ground cardamom
3 tbsp medium-heat curry powder
400g carton passata
300g new potatoes
300g spinach (tougher stalks
  removed and roughly chopped
  if using large leaf spinach)
A bunch of mint, leaves picked and
  roughly chopped
Sea salt and freshly cracked
  black pepper

First, make the paneer. Slowly bring the milk to a simmer
and stir in 2 tbsp lemon juice and the salt. The milk should
start to split quite quickly, but keep stirring and add more
lemon juice, bit by bit, until the milk has fully separated
into curds and whey. The amount of lemon juice you need
will vary depending on the freshness of the milk.

Line a sieve with a double layer of muslin and set it over a
bowl. Pour the cheese mixture into the sieve and leave for
about 10 minutes to allow the whey to drain through the
cloth. Draw the muslin up around the paneer and gently
squeeze out any excess liquid. You should have about
650g paneer.

Transfer the cloth-wrapped paneer to a tray and pat it
out to a 2cm thickness. Cover it with a tray and weigh
down with a couple of heavy tins. Place in the fridge for
at least 2 hours.

To prepare the filling, place a large saucepan over a low
heat and add the rapeseed oil. When it is hot, toss in the
onions, ginger and garlic and cook gently for at least
45 minutes until very soft and golden brown (this long,
slow cooking really deepen the flavours in the final dish).

Once the onion mixture is lovely and soft, add all of the
spices and cook, stirring frequently, for 3–4 minutes.
(Don't be tempted to raise the heat, as the spices will
burn and turn bitter.) If the mixture seems dry when the
spices go in, add a little extra oil.

continued overleaf

Add the passata to the spiced onion mix, stir well and bring to a simmer. Cook for at least 15 minutes, stirring frequently to prevent the sauce sticking.

While the curry sauce is simmering, add the new potatoes to a pan of lightly salted water, bring back to a simmer and cook for 15–20 minutes until they are just cooked in the centre. Drain and allow to cool a little, then cut in half.

Preheat the oven to 210°C/190°C Fan/Gas 6½ and line a baking tray with baking paper. Dice the paneer into rough 1cm chunks.

Once the curry sauce has cooked for long enough, add the potatoes and paneer and stir well, then start adding the spinach a handful at a time, stirring to encourage the leaves to wilt down. Once all of the spinach is combined, stir through the chopped mint. Now taste and season the mixture accordingly with salt and pepper. Leave to cool.

Roll out the shortcrust pastry on a lightly floured surface to a rectangle, roughly 30 x 20cm and no thinner than 5mm. Brush the outer 2cm with egg wash.

Pile the filling onto the middle of the pastry and spread out evenly into a smaller rectangle, about 15 x 10cm. Bring the long sides of the pastry up over the filling and lightly press them together. Now fold the shorter ends exactly as you would wrap a present to seal in the filling.

Carefully lift the pie and flip it over onto the lined tray, so the seams are underneath. Brush the pastry with egg wash and make 3–4 slashes along the top. Bake in the oven for 25–30 minutes until the pastry is golden brown. Serve hot from the oven.

Summer veg satay pie

Wonderfully spicy, nutty satay sauce really lifts crunchy summer veg and nobody will be expecting to find this combination beneath a pie crust! By adding the tomatoes at the last minute you'll find them still whole when you dig in, so you still get that pop of pure summer brilliance. We are spoilt with great produce in the summer so don't get too hung up on the veg combo; as long as you have roughly the same total weight you can just buy what's looking great.

Serves 4–6

500g shortcrust (page 16) or
 rough puff pastry (page 28)
Flour, to dust
Egg wash (beaten egg)

For the filling
2 small courgettes
4 spring onions
1 red pepper, cored and deseeded
150g mangetout or sugar snap
 peas
3 tbsp cold-pressed rapeseed oil
250g cherry tomatoes
200g spinach (tougher stalks
 removed and roughly chopped
 if using large leaf spinach)
Sea salt and freshly cracked
 black pepper

For the satay sauce
Finely grated zest and juice of
 1 lime
1 tsp honey
1 tbsp tamari or soy sauce
1 tbsp curry powder
3 tbsp crunchy peanut butter
400ml tin coconut milk

Preheat the oven to 220°C/200°C Fan/Gas 7.

To prepare the filling, cut the courgettes, spring onions and red pepper into 2cm pieces and put them into a roasting tray with the mangetout or sugar snaps. Trickle over the rapeseed oil, season with salt and pepper and tumble together. Roast in the oven for 5 minutes. Take out the tray, add the cherry tomatoes and give everything a stir. Return to the oven for 3 minutes.

Meanwhile, put all the satay sauce ingredients into a pan and heat gently, stirring to combine, until the sauce is nice and thick. Season with salt and pepper to taste.

Take the roasting tray from the oven and add the spinach, a handful at a time, stirring it through the other veg until fully wilted. Pour the satay sauce over the veg and stir gently to mix. Transfer to a pie dish or roasting tin, about 25 x 20cm, and leave to cool.

Roll out the pastry on a lightly floured surface until slightly larger all round than your pie dish and no thinner than 5mm. Drape loosely over the veg filling and press the edges onto the rim of the dish. Trim away the excess and crimp the edges.

Brush the pie lid with egg wash, pierce in a few places and bake in the oven for 20 minutes until the pastry is golden brown. Serve hot from the oven.

Cauliflower cheese filo pie

Who doesn't love cauliflower cheese? Even better, this one has a trio of cheeses: classic rich Cheddar, stringy mozzarella and smoked cheese for depth. This recipe uses the entire cauli – stalks, leaves and all – roasting it to ramp up that gorgeous brassica nuttiness. Encasing the cauliflower cheese in filo gives it a light, crunchy pastry element. Irresistible!

Serves 4

5 filo pastry sheets, about 300g
   in total (page 37)
Olive oil, to brush

For the filling
250g medium new potatoes
1 medium cauliflower
2 tbsp cold-pressed rapeseed oil
150g smoked cheese, sliced
150g Cheddar, grated
1 ball of mozzarella (125g), torn
   into small pieces
A small bunch of chives,
   finely chopped
Sea salt and freshly cracked
   black pepper

Preheat the oven to 190°C/170°C Fan/Gas 5 and oil a 20cm square (or 22cm round) loose-bottomed cake tin.

For the filling, add the potatoes to a pan of salted water and bring to the boil then lower the heat and simmer for 15–20 minutes until just cooked. Drain in a colander and allow to steam-dry and cool. Once cooled, cut into slices.

Break off the leaves from the cauliflower, slice the big ribs from the leaves and finely dice these; finely slice the leafy parts. Break the cauli into medium florets; dice the stalk.

Put the cauliflower florets and stalk on a shallow roasting tray. Trickle over the rapeseed oil, season with salt and pepper and tumble together. Roast for 8–12 minutes until starting to soften, then remove from the oven and toss through the leaves. Leave to cool for a few minutes.

Drape a sheet of filo into the oiled cake tin to line the base and sides, allowing it to overhang the rim of the tin, and brush the pastry with oil. Layer another 3 sheets in the tin, slightly off-centre so you have plenty of overhang to cover the top, brushing each with oil. Arrange a layer of potato slices over the pastry base and season lightly.

Tumble the cauliflower, remaining potato slices, cheeses and chives together in a bowl and season, bearing in mind that cheese adds salt. Pile into the tin and cover with the final filo sheet. Fold the overhanging filo over the top.

Brush the surface with oil and bake for 15–20 minutes until golden. Serve hot or at room temperature.

Split pea dhal
and roast root veg pie

Dhal is one of my favourite things to eat and topping it with pastry gives you the perfect vehicle to mop up the spicy filling. I'm using English split peas here rather than imported lentils; otherwise it's a classic dhal recipe.

Serves 4–6

500g shortcrust (page 16) or
   rough puff pastry (page 28)
Flour, to dust
Egg wash (beaten egg)

For the dhal
300g yellow split peas, washed
   and soaked for 30 minutes
1 cinnamon stick
2 tsp ground turmeric
55g fresh ginger: 25g sliced;
   30g finely grated
1 red chilli, split lengthways
3 tbsp sunflower oil
1 medium onion, finely chopped
2 garlic cloves, finely chopped
2 tsp ground cumin
1 tsp ground coriander
1 tsp garam masala
200g passata
Juice of 2 lemons
Sea salt and freshly cracked
   black pepper

For the roast veg
2 carrots
1 parsnip
150g celeriac
150g shallots, halved
3 tbsp cold-pressed rapeseed oil

Preheat the oven to 200°C/180°C Fan/Gas 6.

To make the dhal, drain the split peas and place in a large saucepan with the cinnamon, turmeric, sliced ginger and chilli. Cover with water and bring to a simmer. Cook over a medium heat, stirring often to avoid sticking, for about 25 minutes until the peas are cooked. Add water as you need to (rather than start with a lot); you should have almost no liquid at the end of cooking. Remove the chilli, cinnamon and ginger and drain off any liquid that remains.

Meanwhile, place another saucepan over a medium heat and add the sunflower oil. When hot, toss in the onion, garlic and grated ginger and cook for about 30 minutes until soft and caramelised. Add the cumin, coriander and garam masala and cook, stirring, for a few minutes. Add the passata and simmer for 10 minutes.

While the dhal is cooking, cut the root veg into 2–3cm chunks. Tip onto a shallow roasting tray with the shallots. Trickle over the rapeseed oil, season and tumble together. Roast in the oven for 20–25 minutes until nicely coloured.

Once cooked, combine the split peas and spiced tomato mix. Add the lemon juice and seasoning to taste. Stir the roasted veg through the dhal and check the seasoning again. Tip into a pie dish, about 25 x 20cm; leave to cool.

Roll out the pastry on a lightly floured surface until slightly larger all round than your dish and no thinner than 5mm. Drape over the pie dish and press the edges onto the rim. Trim away the excess and crimp the edges. Brush with egg wash, pierce in a few places and cook for 25 minutes until the pastry is golden brown. Serve hot from the oven.

Merguez spiced squash, chickpea and apricot pie

Merguez spice is one of my favourite seasonings. I make it in bulk and store it in jars because any veg you're cooking will benefit from a sprinkle. Butternut is lovely in this recipe, but if you can get your hands on a funkier squash, like a Crown Prince, try it. Unsulphured dried apricots are a must – they have a much richer flavour than their bright orange counterparts.

Serves 4

250g rough puff pastry (page 28)
Flour, to dust
Egg wash (beaten egg)

For the merguez spice blend
1 tbsp cumin seed
1 tbsp coriander seeds
1 tbsp fennel seeds
1 tbsp caraway seeds
1 tbsp sweet paprika
½ tsp cayenne pepper, or to taste

For the filling
3 small red onions, quartered
4 tbsp cold-pressed rapeseed oil
1kg squash, such as butternut or
    Crown Prince, deseeded
3 garlic cloves, finely sliced
400g tin chickpeas, drained
400g tin chopped tomatoes
1 tbsp tomato purée
100g dried apricots (unsulphured),
    roughly chopped
100ml coconut milk
A small bunch of coriander, leaves
    picked and roughly chopped
A small bunch of mint, leaves
    picked and roughly chopped
Sea salt and freshly cracked
    black pepper

Preheat the oven to 210°C/190°C Fan/Gas 6½.

To make the spice blend, scatter the whole seeds on a roasting tray and toast in the oven for 4–5 minutes. Take out, let cool slightly and then grind using a pestle and mortar or spice blender, keeping some texture. Mix with the paprika, cayenne and a little black pepper.

For the filling, place the onions in a large roasting tray, pour over half of the rapeseed oil and tumble together. Roast in the oven for 20 minutes. Meanwhile, peel the squash and cut into 2–3cm cubes.

Remove the tray from the oven and add the squash, garlic, 2–3 tbsp of the spice blend and the rest of the oil. Toss well and return to the oven for 25 minutes, turning the veg halfway. The squash will have started to soften.

In a large bowl, mix together the chickpeas, tinned tomatoes, tomato purée, chopped apricots, coconut milk and chopped herbs. Add the roasted squash mix and season with salt and pepper. Now taste and add more spice if you think it needs it. Tip the filling into a deep pie dish or roasting dish, about 25 x 20cm.

Roll out the pastry on a lightly floured surface until slightly larger all round than your dish and no thinner than 5mm. Drape over the filling and press the edges onto the rim of the dish. Trim away the excess and crimp the edges.

Brush with egg wash and bake for 35–40 minutes until the pastry is golden and crispy. Serve hot from the oven.

Mushroom, chestnut and stout steamed pudding

I've made this for lots of people over the years and it's always gone down well – with meat eaters as well as my vegetarian family. If you don't want the faff of a pudding, the deliciously rich filling makes an equally great pie. I like to use a good variety of mushrooms and always include some big flat field mushrooms. If you're lucky enough to be able to source some wild mushrooms they'll add a really good boost of flavour.

Serves 6

For the filling
1.5kg mixed mushrooms
3 tbsp cold-pressed rapeseed oil
2 medium onions, finely chopped
2 carrots, finely chopped
2 celery sticks, finely chopped
2 garlic cloves, finely chopped
3 tbsp tamari or soy sauce
2 tbsp miso
1 tbsp dried seaweed flakes
    (optional)
330ml stout
330ml light ale, such as IPA
5 sprigs of thyme
2 bay leaves
A small bunch of tarragon, leaves
    picked and finely chopped
About 1 tbsp cornflour, mixed to
    a paste with a little cold water
Sea salt and freshly cracked
    black pepper

For the pastry
1kg freshly made suet pastry
    (page 40)
Butter, to grease
Flour, to dust
Egg wash (beaten egg; optional)

First prepare the filling. Finely slice one-third of the mushrooms; cut the rest of them into large chunks, or leave whole if small, and set aside.

Place a large saucepan over a medium heat and add the rapeseed oil. When hot, add the onions, carrots, celery, sliced mushrooms and garlic. Cook, stirring, until the veg start to soften, then turn up the heat so they take on a good brown colour. Add the rest of the mushrooms and cook until they soften and take on colour.

Add the tamari or soy, miso, seaweed if using, stout, ale, thyme, bay leaves and tarragon. Bring to a simmer and cook for 30 minutes, stirring occasionally until the liquor starts to reduce. Slowly trickle in the cornflour paste, stirring as you do so, until the sauce thickens (you may not need it all).

Grease and flour a 1 litre pudding basin. Following the instructions on page 43, line the basin with two-thirds of the suet pastry. Spoon in the filling, cover with the remaining pastry and seal the pastry edges.

Cover the basin with a pleated sheet of foil, securing it with string under the rim. Stand the basin on a small plate or trivet in a large, deep pan and pour in enough boiling water to come halfway up its sides. Put the lid on the pan and bring to a simmer over a medium heat. Steam the pud for 45 minutes, topping up the boiling water as necessary.

Lift out the basin and remove the foil. Loosen the sides of the pudding with a knife, then invert onto a warmed plate.

Spicy parsnip and kale pie

Parsnips just love curry spices. Their brilliant sweetness means they can take a hefty spice hit that would otherwise make a dish a little bitter. The smaller the parsnips you can find the better, but if you can only get hold of big ones, split them lengthways into quarters and cut out the hard core as this can be incredibly tough in older veg. I love to use cavolo nero, but any greens will do – spinach, chard or spring greens are all good here.

Serves 4–6

500g shortcrust (page 16) or
  rough puff pastry (page 28)
Egg wash (beaten egg)

For the filling
750g parsnips, cut into 3cm pieces
3 small red onions, quartered
4 tbsp sunflower oil
4 garlic cloves, sliced
2 tsp ground cumin
1 tsp ground coriander
1 tsp ground turmeric
1 tsp nigella seeds
1 tsp fennel seeds
2 tbsp medium-heat curry powder
250g cavolo nero, kale or other
  leafy green veg, coarse stalks
  removed, roughly chopped
500ml hot veg stock
A bunch of coriander, leaves picked
  and roughly chopped
About 1 tbsp cornflour, mixed to
  a paste with a little cold water
Sea salt and freshly cracked
  black pepper

Preheat the oven to 200°C/180°C Fan/Gas 6.

Put the parsnips and onions into a roasting dish. Trickle over 1 tbsp sunflower oil, season with salt and pepper and roast in the oven for 25 minutes until the parsnips are starting to soften.

Place a medium saucepan over a medium heat and add the remaining 3 tbsp oil. Add the garlic and all of the spices and cook for a couple of minutes, stirring constantly to avoid the spices burning.

Add the cavolo or kale to the saucepan and pour in the stock. Bring to a simmer and cook for a few minutes until the veg is tender, then stir through the coriander. Trickle the cornflour paste into the pan, stirring as you do so, until the sauce is nice and thick (you may not need it all).

Remove the roasted veg from the oven, add to the spicy sauce and stir through. Tip into a roasting tin, about 25 x 20cm and 8cm deep, and leave to cool down.

Roll out the pastry on a lightly floured surface until it is slightly larger all round than your roasting tin and no thinner than 5mm.

Drape the pastry over the filling and gently press the edges onto the sides of the tin. Trim away the excess and crimp the edges. Brush with egg wash and pierce a couple of times. Cook in the oven for 25–30 minutes until golden brown. Serve hot from the oven.

3
OPEN PIES
& TARTS

We all know a good quiche can be truly delicious and I hope you'll try my recipe overleaf, boldly entitled 'the ultimate'. I've spent some time honing it to perfection and I don't think you will be disappointed!

The idea of making tarts may seem a bit challenging, but I promise you they are not difficult. If you follow the steps in the first chapter and nail making a pastry case, tarts will become effortless and you'll be knocking them out just for fun.

I love the classics and there is no beating my sister Melle's homity pie on page 88, which has a pastry recipe all of its own, full of cheese and herbs. If you like it here, try using it with other savoury pie and tart recipes in the book.

I haven't just given you classic shortcrust pastry tarts, there are also some stunning rough puff pastry tarts and savoury galettes, which are really open pies constructed to reveal their tempting fillings. So, whatever your time frame, there's something to choose from here.

Whether it's a formal affair or just a snack for the weekend, the recipes in this chapter will fit the bill. They look great, taste great and show everyone that a quiche can be a thing of wonder!

The ultimate quiche

I wouldn't label something as 'the ultimate' lightly, but I think this really deserves the title. A good quiche can be a thing of wonder, but it is often confused with its inferior shop-bought cousin. This recipe, with its beautiful biscuity pastry case and deliciously rich filling, will enable you to appreciate what a real quiche is! For me, the simplicity of caramelised onions is what makes it the best, but you can add any veg into the creamy egg mix to make wonderful quiches forever more.

Serves 4–6

300g shortcrust pastry (page 16)
Flour, to dust
Egg wash (beaten egg)

For the filling
500g onions, sliced
3 garlic cloves, finely sliced
3 tbsp extra virgin olive oil
A small bunch of flat-leaf parsley,
 leaves picked and chopped
300g mature Cheddar, grated
3 medium eggs
200ml double cream
Sea salt and freshly cracked
 black pepper

Preheat the oven to 180°C/160°C Fan/Gas 4.

Roll out the pastry on a lightly floured surface and use to line a 20cm tart tin, 4cm deep, placed on a baking sheet (as described on page 24). Prick the pastry, line with baking paper and baking beans and bake blind, then trim and seal (as detailed on page 27).

To prepare the filling, place a saucepan over a low heat and add the onions, garlic and olive oil. Cook slowly, stirring occasionally, for 30–45 minutes until the onions are completely softened and sweet. Add the chopped parsley and season with salt and pepper to taste.

Tip the onion mix into the tart case and scatter over the grated cheese. Carefully mix through the onions.

In a bowl, beat the eggs and cream together briefly until just combined (you don't want to aerate the mix). Season with salt and pepper and carefully pour over the filling in the tart case, making sure you don't spill any down the sides.

Carefully transfer the quiche to the oven and bake for 35–40 minutes until the filling is just set.

Leave to stand for 5 minutes then carefully remove the quiche from the tin. Serve hot from the oven or at room temperature, with a leafy salad on the side.

Spiced shallot, bean and mozzarella tarts

These spicy little numbers are great eaten hot from the oven or cooled and packed away for lunch or a picnic. Make sure you push a good helping of cheese into each tart, as the creamy mozzarella really makes these special. I use tinned ready-cooked beans for convenience – use any combo of beans you fancy. And, as always with chilli, up the heat or lower it, according to your tolerance.

Makes 6

500g shortcrust pastry (page 16)
Flour, to dust
Egg wash (beaten egg)

For the filling
2 balls of mozzarella (125g each)
250g shallots, halved
3 garlic cloves, sliced
4 sprigs of thyme
4 tbsp extra virgin olive oil
1 medium-heat red chilli, deseeded
    and finely diced
2 tsp ground cumin
200g passata
400g tin mixed beans, drained
    and rinsed
200g cherry vine tomatoes
Sea salt and freshly cracked
    black pepper

Preheat the oven to 180°C/160°C Fan/Gas 4.

Roll out the pastry on a lightly floured surface and use to line six individual 10cm tart tins placed on a baking sheet (as described on page 24). Prick the pastry, line with baking paper and baking beans and bake blind for 15 minutes, then trim and seal (as detailed on page 27).

For the filling, tear the mozzarella into pieces, place in a sieve and leave to drain for at least 30 minutes.

Turn the oven up to 200°C/180°C Fan/Gas 6. Put the shallots, garlic and thyme into a roasting tray. Trickle over the olive oil, season with salt and pepper and tumble everything together. Roast in the oven for 20 minutes, stirring halfway through.

Take out the roasting tray, add the chilli, cumin, passata, beans and cherry tomatoes and give everything a good stir. Return to the oven and cook for a further 10 minutes, stirring halfway through. Remove and taste for seasoning; adjust accordingly. Allow to cool.

Spoon the spiced veg mixture into the tart cases and divide the mozzarella between them, pushing it into the filling. Bake in the oven for 10–15 minutes until the cheese is melted.

Leave to stand for a few minutes then carefully remove the tarts from the tins. Serve hot or at room temperature, with lots of peppery leaves.

Roast courgette, pepper and fennel galette

This classic combination of roasted veg is a favourite for good reason: it's absolutely delicious. Through the cooking process, the veg should gain some crispy, dark edges, which enhance the flavour. Try to find a soft goat's cheese that doesn't have a rind – Rosary goat's cheese, which is produced near Salisbury, is an excellent choice.

Serves 6

500g shortcrust (page 16) or
  rough puff pastry (page 32)
Flour, to dust
Egg wash (beaten egg)

For the filling
2 medium courgettes
2 red or yellow peppers, halved,
  cored and deseeded
200g fennel, trimmed
3 garlic cloves, roughly chopped
3 tbsp extra virgin olive oil
100g sun-dried tomatoes, roughly
  chopped (any oil saved)
4 sprigs of thyme
A generous bunch of basil, leaves
  picked and torn
150g soft goat's cheese
Sea salt and freshly cracked
  black pepper

Preheat the oven to 210°C/190°C Fan/Gas 6½ and line a baking tray with baking paper.

For the filling, cut the courgettes, peppers and fennel into 2cm pieces and place on a shallow roasting tray with the garlic. Trickle over the olive oil and any oil from the sun-dried tomatoes. Roast in the oven for 15 minutes, tossing the veg halfway through. Remove and leave to cool.

Roll out the pastry on a lightly floured surface to a 5mm thickness and trim to a rough round, about 35cm in diameter. Lift the pastry round onto the lined baking tray and brush the outer 2cm with egg wash.

Toss the sun-dried tomatoes, thyme sprigs and basil through the roast veg then pile the filling onto the middle of the pastry round, leaving a 6–8cm clear border. Dot the goat's cheese evenly around the veg.

Fold the pastry edges up and partially over the filling, leaving the middle exposed so you can see it. As you fold the edges up, press the creases together to stop the pastry unfolding.

Brush the exposed pastry with egg wash and bake in the oven for 25–30 minutes until golden brown. Serve hot from the oven or at room temperature.

Asparagus, roast garlic and green herb tart

Asparagus is probably my favourite veg and during its short season I'll eat it almost every day. The closer you can get to the point it's been picked, the better the eating experience. As for the garlic, I often roast quite a lot in one go so I have the wonderful purée to hand to flavour all manner of dishes. It lasts for up to 10 days in the fridge and freezes well, too.

Serves 6

400g shortcrust pastry (page 16)
Flour, to dust
Egg wash (beaten egg)

For the filling
2 garlic bulbs
2 tbsp extra virgin olive oil
500g asparagus spears, trimmed
    and cut into 2.5cm lengths
A small bunch of flat-leaf parsley,
    leaves picked and finely chopped
A small bunch of chives, finely
    chopped
A small bunch of dill, leaves picked
    and finely chopped
3 medium eggs
200ml double cream
150g mature Cheddar, grated
Sea salt and freshly cracked
    black pepper

Preheat the oven to 180°C/160°C Fan/Gas 4.

Roll out the pastry on a lightly floured surface and use to line a 23cm square or 25cm round tart tin, 4cm deep, placed on a baking sheet (as described on page 24). Prick the pastry, line with baking paper and baking beans and bake blind, then trim and seal (as detailed on page 27).

Turn the oven up to 190°C/170°C Fan/Gas 5. Place the garlic bulbs on a sheet of foil, season with salt and pepper and trickle over half the olive oil. Wrap tightly and place in the oven for 45–60 minutes until tender (you should be able to squidge the garlic in the foil). Remove from the oven and allow to cool.

Place the asparagus on a roasting tray, trickle over the rest of the olive oil and season with salt and pepper. Cook in the oven for 3–4 minutes to partially soften.

Tip all of the herbs into a bowl. Slice off a small sliver from the bottom of each garlic bulb and then squeeze out the soft roasted garlic into the bowl, discarding the skin. Add the eggs and cream and whisk together. Add half of the grated cheese and season well with salt and pepper.

Scatter the rest of the cheese in the pastry case and then carefully pour on the creamy mixture. Arrange the asparagus evenly in the pastry case. Bake in the oven for 30 minutes until the filling is just set in the centre; to test, pierce with a knife and check for any runny egg. Leave to stand for 5 minutes then carefully remove from the tin. Serve hot or warm.

Caramelised onion and smoked Cheddar tart

Smoked Cheddar is one of my favourite cheeses and Dorset Red is a delicious version produced down the road from us in West Dorset. I'm using plenty of it here, along with sweet onions and a good hit of thyme, to make an indulgent filling. Make this tart once and I promise you'll make it again! It rarely has time to cool down in our house, but if it does it will be delicious in a packed lunch.

Serves 6

300g shortcrust pastry (page 16)
Flour, to dust
Egg wash (beaten egg)

For the filling
2 tbsp cold-pressed rapeseed oil
3 medium onions, sliced
3 garlic cloves, sliced
3 sprigs of thyme
3 medium eggs
100ml whole milk
100ml double cream
200g smoked Cheddar, grated
Sea salt and freshly cracked
   black pepper

Preheat the oven to 180°C/160°C Fan/Gas 4.

Roll out the pastry on a lightly floured surface and use to line a 20cm loose-bottomed tart tin, 4cm deep, placed on a baking sheet (as described on page 24). Prick the pastry, line with baking paper and baking beans and bake blind, then trim and seal (as detailed on page 27).

Turn the oven up to 190°C/170°C Fan/Gas 5.

For the filling, place a saucepan over a medium heat and add the rapeseed oil. When hot, add the onions along with the garlic and thyme and cook, stirring, for 15 minutes or so, until soft and golden brown. Pick out and discard the thyme stalks.

In a bowl, beat the eggs, milk and cream together until smoothly combined. Season with salt and pepper and stir through the grated cheese.

Spoon the onion mixture into the tart case and spread out evenly, then carefully pour over the creamy egg mix. Bake in the oven for 35–40 minutes until the filling is just cooked in the centre.

Leave to stand for 5 minutes then carefully remove the tart from the tin. Serve hot from the oven or at room temperature, with a leafy salad on the side.

Broccoli, goat's cheese and almond puff tart

Broccoli is one of the most frequently purchased vegetables in the UK, but most of it is imported. Homegrown purple sprouting is the best option. It has two lengthy seasons: early spring through to early summer and autumn through to Christmas. At other times, look for tenderstem and standard broccoli that's been grown in this country.

Serves 6

500g rough puff pastry (page 28)
Flour, to dust
Egg wash (beaten egg)

For the filling
350g broccoli florets (purple
  sprouting, tenderstem or regular)
250g soft goat's cheese, crumbled
2 medium eggs, beaten
Finely grated zest of 1 lemon
A small bunch of coriander, leaves
  picked and roughly chopped
100g almonds (skin on),
  roughly chopped
Sea salt and freshly cracked
  black pepper

Preheat the oven to 220°C/200°C Fan/Gas 7 and line a baking sheet with baking paper.

To prepare the filling, bring a pan of lightly salted water to the boil, add the broccoli and cook for 3–4 minutes. Drain, then spread out in a single layer on a tray and allow to cool.

Mix the goat's cheese and beaten eggs together in a bowl. Add the broccoli florets, lemon zest, chopped coriander and almonds, toss to mix and season well with salt and pepper.

Set aside a quarter of the pastry. Roll out the rest of the pastry to a 30 x 25cm rectangle, about 5mm thick, and trim to neaten. Place on the lined baking sheet and brush the outer 2cm with egg wash.

Roll out the remaining pastry to a 5mm thick oblong. Cut 2cm wide strips to fit on the egg-washed edges of the first rectangle, position them and press gently to adhere. Brush this pastry border with egg wash. Prick the pastry within the border with a fork.

Spoon the broccoli filling over the pastry base within the raised border and bake in the oven for 20 minutes or until the filling is set in the middle and golden brown. Serve hot from the oven or at room temperature.

Melle's homity pie

Melle is one of my older sisters and a very good cook, too. So, it's with no shame that I'm stealing her recipe for the age-old homity pie – typically filled with almost-mashed potato, cheese and basil. She's taken the pie on a bit of a journey, giving the filling more texture and packing the pastry with cheese and herbs. You can use it for almost any savoury tart or pie.

Serves 6–8

For the pastry
125g plain flour, plus extra to dust
125g fine wholemeal flour
A pinch of salt
125g cold butter, diced
125g mature Cheddar, grated
A bunch of flat-leaf parsley, leaves
    picked and finely chopped
1 tsp English mustard
1 tsp poppy seeds
2 medium eggs, beaten, plus
    extra for egg wash

For the filling
750g floury potatoes, such as
    Maris Piper or King Edward,
    peeled and quartered
2 tbsp extra virgin olive oil
3 leeks, trimmed and sliced
80g butter, cut into cubes
200g mature Cheddar
    (the stronger the better), grated
A generous bunch of basil or
    oregano, leaves picked and
    roughly torn
Sea salt and freshly cracked
    black pepper

To make the pastry, mix the flours and salt together in a large bowl, add the butter and rub in with your fingers until the mixture is the texture of fine breadcrumbs. Mix in the cheese, parsley, mustard, poppy seeds and eggs. Gather into a ball, turn out and knead for 2–3 minutes to form a smooth, slightly sticky dough. Form into a disc, wrap tightly and rest in the fridge for 45 minutes.

Preheat the oven to 180°C/160°C Fan/Gas 4. Grease and flour a 25cm loose-bottomed tart tin, 3cm deep, and place on a baking sheet. Roll out the pastry on a lightly floured surface to a 3–4mm thickness and use to line the tart tin (as described on page 24). Prick the pastry, line with baking paper and baking beans and bake blind, then trim and seal (as detailed on page 27).

Make the filling while the tart case is baking. Steam or boil the potatoes until cooked through, about 15–20 minutes, then drain and leave to steam-dry for a few minutes.

Place a saucepan over a medium heat and add the olive oil. Toss in the leeks and sweat for 5–7 minutes until nice and soft. Take off the heat and add the potatoes with the butter, 150g of the cheese and most of the basil/oregano. Stir to melt the butter and break up the potatoes a bit. Season with salt and pepper and mix until well combined.

Turn the oven up to 210°C/190°C Fan/Gas 6½. Spread the filling evenly in the tart case. Scatter over the remaining cheese and herbs. Bake in the oven for 25–30 minutes until the cheese is bubbling and golden. Leave to stand for 5 minutes then carefully remove from the tin and serve.

Roast squash, red onion, apple and blue cheese galette

When you pop this galette-style pie on the table, everyone can see the lovely caramelised veg with their crispy dark edges. I like to use a strong, salty blue cheese but if you're not a fan or you just fancy something milder, this works with literally any other cheese.

Serves 6

500g rough puff (page 28) or
    shortcrust pastry (page 16)
Flour, to dust
Egg wash (beaten egg)

For the filling
1 medium squash (1.5–2kg), peeled
    (if necessary), deseeded and cut
    into 2–3cm wedges
5 medium red onions, halved
12 sage leaves, sliced into ribbons
6 sprigs of thyme, leaves picked
4 tbsp olive oil
6 garlic cloves
2 apples, halved, cored and cut
    into wedges
25g pumpkin seeds
150g blue cheese, crumbled
Sea salt and freshly cracked
    black pepper

Preheat the oven to 200°C/180°C Fan/Gas 6 and line a baking tray with baking paper.

For the filling, lay the squash wedges and onion halves on a shallow roasting tray. Scatter over the herbs, trickle over the olive oil and season with salt and pepper. Bash the garlic cloves lightly and add these too. Roast in the oven for 25 minutes.

Take out the tray, add the apple wedges and pumpkin seeds and give everything a stir. Return to the oven for 10 minutes then remove and leave to cool.

Roll out the pastry on a lightly floured surface to a 5mm thickness and trim to a rough round, about 35cm in diameter. Lift the pastry round onto the lined baking tray and brush the outer 2cm with egg wash.

Once the veg is cooked, tumble the blue cheese through and then spoon onto the pastry round, leaving a 6–8cm clear border. Fold the pastry edges up and partially over the filling, leaving the middle exposed so you can see all the lovely ingredients. As you fold the edges up, press the creases together to stop the pastry unfolding.

Brush the exposed pastry with egg wash and bake in the oven for 25–30 minutes until the pastry is golden brown. Serve hot from the oven or at room temperature.

Courgette, sun-dried tomato and pumpkin seed tart

The pumpkin seed cream used here is a great way to create a creamy filling that's more interesting than just dairy, with the added sumac and chilli lending a hot, citrussy note. Courgettes are one of my favourite veg and slicing them thinly for this tart ensures they cook nice and quickly.

Serves 6–8

500g rough puff pastry (page 28)
Flour, to dust
Egg wash (beaten egg)

For the pumpkin seed cream
100g pumpkin seeds
1 tsp sumac
½ small chilli, deseeded
3 tbsp sunflower oil

For the filling
2 small courgettes
A small handful of dill, leaves
  picked and finely chopped
1 tsp fennel seeds
1 tbsp extra virgin olive oil
200g sun-dried tomatoes,
  roughly chopped
Sea salt and freshly cracked
  black pepper

Preheat the oven to 220°C/200°C Fan/Gas 7 and line a baking sheet with baking paper.

For the pumpkin seed cream, put the pumpkin seeds, sumac and chilli into a saucepan, cover with water and cook gently, topping up the water if necessary, for about 25 minutes until the pumpkin seeds soften. Put the seeds and chilli into a jug blender with some of the cooking liquor and blitz, adding more of the liquid as necessary to achieve a thick sauce consistency (if it is all used, water will do). Then, with the motor running, trickle in the sunflower oil to make a light, silky cream. Season to taste.

For the filling, thinly slice the courgettes lengthways. Place in a bowl with the chopped dill, fennel seeds, olive oil and some salt and pepper. Tumble together.

Set aside a quarter of the pastry. Roll out the rest of the pastry to a 30 x 25cm rectangle, about 5mm thick, and trim to neaten. Place on the lined baking sheet and brush the outer 2cm with egg wash.

Roll out the remaining pastry to a 5mm thick oblong. Cut 2cm wide strips to fit on the egg-washed edges of the first rectangle, position them and press gently to adhere. Brush this pastry border with egg wash. Prick the pastry within the border with a fork.

Spread the pumpkin seed cream over the pastry within the border. Distribute the sun-dried tomatoes over the cream and layer the courgette ribbons on top. Bake for 20 minutes until the pastry is deep golden brown at the edges. Serve hot from the oven or at room temperature.

Three cheese, leek and new potato open pie

As a kid, one of my favourite dinners was cheese and potato pie, with a simple filling of mash and Cheddar. Now I prefer to use bashed new potatoes with their skins on and a mixture of cheeses. Here I've included mature Cheddar, blue and smoked cheese, but whatever you have to hand will do. As long as you have lots of cheese you'll be in for a treat.

Serves 6

500g rough puff (page 28) or
   shortcrust pastry (page 16)
Flour, to dust
Egg wash (beaten egg)

For the filling
750g new potatoes
3 tbsp extra virgin olive oil
3 leeks, trimmed and sliced
3 garlic cloves, sliced
A bunch of flat-leaf parsley, leaves
   picked and finely chopped
1 tbsp sumac
Finely grated zest of 1 lemon
100g mature Cheddar, grated
100g blue cheese, crumbled
100g smoked Cheddar, grated
Sea salt and freshly cracked
   black pepper

For the filling, add the new potatoes to a saucepan of lightly salted water, bring to a simmer and cook for 15–20 minutes until they are just cooked. Drain in a colander and allow to steam-dry.

Place the saucepan back over a medium heat and add the olive oil. When hot, add the leeks and garlic and cook, stirring occasionally, until they start to soften. Add the chopped parsley, sumac and lemon zest and cook for another couple of minutes.

Tip the new potatoes into a bowl and break each one with the back of a fork. Add the leek mixture and all of the cheeses. Mix together well, then taste and season accordingly. Leave to cool.

Preheat the oven to 200°C/180°C Fan/Gas 6 and line a baking sheet with baking paper.

Roll out the pastry on a lightly floured surface to a 5mm thickness and trim to a rough round, about 35cm in diameter. Place on the lined baking sheet and brush the outer 2cm with egg wash.

Spoon the filling evenly onto the pastry round, leaving a 6–8cm clear border. Fold the pastry edges up and partially over the filling, leaving the middle exposed. As you fold the edges up, press the creases together to stop the pastry unfolding.

Brush the exposed pastry with egg wash and bake for 25–30 minutes until golden brown. Serve straight away.

Smoked haddock, spinach and Cheddar tart

Smoked fish tarts have been a personal favourite ever since I started eating fish in my teens (I was a vegetarian up until then). We're lucky enough to have a fishmonger that smokes locally caught fish in Colyton, a village just a stone's throw away, but if you're not so fortunate, look out for naturally smoked fish with the MSC certification, steering clear of anything that's bright yellow. You can use any smoked white fish, including cod and pollock.

Serves 6

300g shortcrust pastry (page 16)
Flour, to dust
Egg wash (beaten egg)

For the filling
400g spinach (tougher stalks
    removed and roughly chopped
    if using large leaf spinach)
180g MSC-certified smoked
    haddock, skinned and diced
150g mature Cheddar, grated
A small bunch of dill, leaves picked
    and finely chopped, plus a few
    extra sprigs to finish
200ml double cream
3 medium eggs
Sea salt and freshly cracked
    black pepper

Preheat the oven to 195°C/175°C Fan/Gas 5.

Roll out the pastry on a lightly floured surface and use to line a loose-bottomed 20cm tart tin, 4cm deep, placed on a baking sheet (as described on page 24). Prick the pastry, line with baking paper and baking beans and bake blind, then trim and seal (as detailed on page 27).

For the filling, place a large saucepan over a high heat, add the spinach and stir continuously until it is fully wilted down. Tip the wilted spinach onto the middle of a clean cloth, gather the cloth around it and twist and squeeze to remove as much moisture as possible, leaving a tightly packed ball.

Put the spinach onto a board and shred it finely, then tip into a large bowl, breaking it up as you do so. Add the diced fish, grated cheese and chopped dill, toss together and season with salt and pepper.

Beat the cream and eggs together in another bowl until just combined, and season well.

Spread the smoked fish and spinach mixture evenly in the tart case and carefully pour on the creamy egg mix. Bake for 40–45 minutes until the filling is just set in the middle.

Leave to stand for 5 minutes then carefully remove from the tin. Serve hot from the oven or at room temperature, scattered with a few fresh dill sprigs.

Roasted red pepper, shallot and chorizo tart

The combination of harissa, chorizo and red pepper in this tart just screams Mediterranean sunshine. Hot and rich with paprika, it takes me back to holidays in Spain, although it's more likely I enjoyed the flavours in a tortilla. But what doesn't a bit of pastry make better?

Serves 4

350g shortcrust pastry (page 16)
Flour, to dust
Egg wash (beaten egg)

For the filling
250g shallots, halved
2 red peppers, halved, cored
    and deseeded
150g cooking chorizo, skinned
    and cut into 1cm cubes
2 tbsp extra virgin olive oil
A small bunch of flat-leaf parsley,
    leaves picked and roughly
    chopped
3 medium eggs
100ml whole milk
100ml double cream
1 tbsp harissa paste
Sea salt and freshly cracked
    black pepper

Preheat the oven to 180°C/160°C Fan/Gas 4.

Roll out the pastry on a lightly floured surface and use to line a 22cm tart tin, 3cm deep, placed on a baking sheet (as described on page 24). Prick the pastry, line with baking paper and baking beans and bake blind, then trim and seal (as detailed on page 27).

Turn the oven up to 210°C/190°C Fan/Gas 6½.

For the filling, put the shallots on a baking tray. Cut each red pepper half into 4 pieces and add to the tray with the chorizo and olive oil. Toss together and roast in the oven for 25 minutes, turning halfway through. Remove from the oven and toss through the chopped parsley.

In a separate bowl, beat the eggs, milk, cream and harissa together until just combined. Season generously with salt and pepper.

Arrange the roasted vegetables in the tart case and pour the creamy egg mix over them. Give the filling a quick swirl to ensure even distribution.

Transfer to the oven and bake for 35–45 minutes until the filling is just cooked in the centre.

Leave the tart to stand for 5 minutes then carefully remove from the tin. Serve hot or at room temperature.

Chicken, smoked chilli and green herb tart

I prefer to use chicken legs for this filling as they are beautifully soft and tender when roasted, unlike chicken breasts which tend to become dry; they are also cheaper. Make sure you use all of the meat, including the skin and adding any jelly. I always have a pot of chipotle chilli flakes in the cupboard; they are usually quite mild but I have been caught out with a couple of hot batches, so beware!

Serves 6

400g shortcrust pastry (page 16)
Flour, to dust
Egg wash (beaten egg)

For the filling
4 large organic or free-range
    chicken legs (thighs and
    drumsticks)
250g shallots, halved
1 tbsp sunflower oil
1 tbsp dried chipotle chilli flakes
A small bunch of flat-leaf parsley,
    leaves picked and finely chopped
A small bunch of chives, finely
    chopped
A small bunch of dill, leaves picked
    and finely chopped
100ml double cream
100ml whole milk
3 medium eggs
Sea salt and freshly cracked
    black pepper

Preheat the oven to 180°C/160°C Fan/Gas 4.

For the filling, put the chicken legs and shallots into a deep roasting dish, trickle over the sunflower oil and toss to coat. Roast in the oven for 1 hour until tender. Remove from the oven and allow to cool.

Meanwhile, roll out the pastry on a lightly floured surface and use to line a 25cm tart tin, 3cm deep, placed on a baking sheet (as described on page 24). Prick the pastry, line with baking paper and baking beans and bake blind, then trim and seal (as detailed on page 27).

Once cooled, pick the chicken from the bones, finely dicing any skin, and place it all in a large bowl with the shallots. Tip in any chicken juices, fat or jelly, along with the chilli flakes and chopped herbs. Toss together and season with salt and pepper.

Beat the cream, milk and eggs together in another bowl until just combined, and season well.

Tip the chicken mixture into the tart case and spread evenly. Carefully pour the egg mixture over the top. Bake in the oven for 35–40 minutes until just set in the centre.

Leave the tart to stand for 5 minutes then carefully remove from the tin. Serve hot from the oven or at room temperature, with a leafy salad on the side.

Ham hock, parsley and mozzarella tart

Ham hocks are underrated things that stay deliciously soft when cooked and can be torn into nice chunks. I've included the cooking instructions for a hock here, but as long as it's good quality, a precooked ham hock will do fine – you'll just miss out on the lovely broth you create when cooking it.

Serves 6

400g shortcrust pastry (page 16)
Flour, to dust
Egg wash (beaten egg)

For the filling
1 ham hock (about 800g)
A generous bunch of flat-leaf
    parsley, stalks separated, leaves
    finely chopped
1 carrot, diced
1 onion, diced
1 celery stick, roughly diced
2 balls of mozzarella (125g each)
100ml double cream
100ml whole milk
3 medium eggs, beaten
1 tsp English mustard
Sea salt and freshly cracked
    black pepper

For the filling, place the ham hock in a large saucepan, cover with cold water and bring to the boil. Taste the liquid and if it is salty, discard and replace with fresh water then bring to the boil again (you can repeat this process a couple of times if necessary). Once the water just has a light salty tang, add the parsley stalks, carrot, onion and celery and simmer for 3–4 hours until the meat is falling away from the bone.

In the meantime, preheat the oven to 180°C/160°C Fan/ Gas 4. Roll out the pastry on a lightly floured surface and use to line a 25cm tart tin, 3cm deep, placed on a baking sheet (as described on page 24). Prick the pastry, line with baking paper and baking beans and bake blind, then trim and seal (as detailed on page 27).

Tear the mozzarella into pieces, place in a sieve and leave to drain for at least 30 minutes. When the ham hock is cooked, remove it from the stock and set aside to cool (save the broth to make soup).

Once cooled, pull the ham off the bone and tear into smaller pieces. Place in a bowl, add the chopped parsley and mix through. In another bowl, beat the cream, milk, eggs and mustard together until just combined, and season with salt and pepper.

Spread the ham mixture in the tart case and dot the torn mozzarella evenly around. Carefully pour on the egg mix and bake in the oven for about 30–35 minutes until just set in the centre. Leave to stand for 5 minutes then carefully remove from the tin. Serve hot from the oven or at room temperature.

4
SAUCY PIES

For me these are the best pies of all – like big hugs coming fresh out of the oven! They emerge with the sauce bubbling up around the golden pastry and glazing it to delicious effect. As you cut through the crunchy crust to the soft interior, steam billows out from the sauce and the hidden aromas – full of promise – are released.

These are the comfort dinners we all love so much. If you're looking for a warming dinner to wow friends or family, this is the chapter to dig into. Check out my Desperate Dan-style beef shin pie on page 109 or the Stargazy pie on page 127 – these are favourites in my house, and I hope they work their way into your homes and hearts, too.

Living up to the chapter title, each recipe is packed full of delicious sauce. The more traditional recipes are enriched with complementary flavours, so even though a chicken and mushroom pie is familiar to all, my recipe on page 106 will feel like a brand-new experience.

Of course, there are a few pies that will be new to you, too. If you have never tasted a meatball pie, here's your chance to try one (see page 118). And the Provençal seafood pie on page 128, featuring beautiful soft fillets of fish under a sweet potato and lemon crust, is a must. Give it a go!

Chicken and mushroom pie

Individual versions of this pie are sold everywhere, from the local chippie to football stadiums, but there's one recurring problem for me: never enough chicken or mushrooms. So here I pack a family-sized pie full of both, and add lots of flavours to the silky sauce that surrounds them.

Serves 4–6

500g shortcrust (page 16) or
   rough puff pastry (page 28)
Flour, to dust
Egg wash (beaten egg)

For the filling
4 large organic or free-range
   chicken legs (thighs and
   drumsticks)
50g unsalted butter
1 onion, diced
3 garlic cloves, chopped
500g flat mushrooms, quartered
50g plain flour
400ml whole milk
100ml white wine
100ml double cream
1 tsp English mustard
A small bunch of flat-leaf parsley,
   leaves picked and chopped
Sea salt and freshly cracked
   black pepper

Preheat the oven to 180°C/160°C Fan/Gas 4.

For the filling, place the chicken legs in a deep roasting tray, season with salt and pepper and cook in the oven for 1 hour. Remove and leave until cool enough to handle. Pick the meat from the bones, finely dicing any skin, and place in a large bowl; keep any juice and fat in the tray. Turn the oven up to 210°C/190°C Fan/Gas 6½.

Melt the butter in a saucepan over a medium heat then add the onion and garlic and cook for 10–15 minutes, until the onion starts to soften. Add the mushrooms and cook for about 5 minutes until they soften.

Stir in the flour, then gradually add the milk, stirring to keep the mixture smooth. Once it is all added, you should have a thick, silky sauce. Add the wine, cream, mustard and parsley, along with any juices from the roasting tray.

Lower the heat and cook the sauce just under a simmer, stirring often, for about 5 minutes. Add the chicken and stir through gently. Taste and season accordingly. Tip into a deep pie dish, about 25 x 15cm, and leave to cool down.

Roll out the pastry on a lightly floured surface until large enough to cover the pie dish generously, and 5mm thick.

Drape the pastry over the filling and press the edges onto the rim of the dish. Trim away the excess pastry and crimp the edges. Brush the pie lid with egg wash and pierce in a couple of places to let steam escape. Bake in the oven for 30 minutes until the pastry is golden brown. Serve straight away, with buttered greens and mash.

Beef and ale pie

Slow-cooked shin is so sticky and unctuous it's the best cut of beef to use in a pie, and with the big shin bone poking proudly through the pastry, this is the perfect show-stopping centrepiece pie. You just might have to speak to your butcher in advance, as the shins are normally boned out as a matter of course. You can use boned-out shin for the pie – the process is just the same but the finish isn't nearly as impressive!

Serves 10–12

750g rough puff pastry (page 28)
Flour, to dust
Egg wash (beaten egg)

For the filling
1 shin of beef on the bone
  (about 4–4.5kg)
1kg shallots, halved
5 garlic cloves, peeled
3 carrots, cut into 2cm pieces
1kg flat mushrooms, quartered
4 sprigs of thyme
2 sprigs of rosemary
4 bay leaves
About 1.2 litres dark ale
2 tbsp English mustard
About 1 tbsp cornflour, mixed to
  a paste with a little cold water
Sea salt and freshly cracked
  black pepper

Preheat the oven to 230°C/220°C Fan/Gas 8.

To prepare the filling, put the shin of beef into a roasting tin, 30cm in diameter and 10cm deep, or a roasting tray, about 34 x 26cm and 10cm deep. Roast in the oven for around 30 minutes until a deep golden-brown colour.

Turn the oven down to 220°C/200°C Fan/Gas 7. Take out the roasting tin or tray, add the shallots, garlic, carrots and mushrooms and give the veg a good stir to coat in the fat released by the meat.

Return to the oven for 15 minutes, stirring the veg every 5 minutes so they take on a little colour. Add the herbs and pour in enough ale to almost fill the tin or tray (but not so full that you're likely to spill it!).

Turn the oven down to 140°C/120°C Fan/Gas 1. Cover the tin or tray with foil, sealing it under the rim, and cook in the oven at this low temperature for at least 10 hours. I suggest doing this overnight while you sleep; this way it won't test your patience and you'll also wake up to the most fabulous smell!

Remove the tin or tray from the oven and check that the meat is very tender – it should be falling off the bone with ease. If it isn't, continue cooking until it does. Once cooked, remove from the oven and carefully transfer the beef shin to another tray.

continued overleaf

When you're ready to assemble the pie, turn the oven up to 220°C/200°C Fan/Gas 7.

Transfer the veg and liquor to a saucepan, add the mustard and bring to a simmer. Slowly trickle in the cornflour paste, stirring as you do so, until the sauce thickens (you may not need it all).

Carefully pick the meat from the shin bone, breaking it into nice big chunks. Add to the sauce, being careful not to break the pieces up too much. Taste and season accordingly with salt and pepper.

Tip the beef filling back into the deep roasting tin or tray and place the shin bone in the centre, thin end up. Leave to cool.

Roll out the pastry on a lightly floured surface to a large round or rectangle (large enough to cover the roasting tin or tray generously). Cut a cross in the centre – large enough for the shin bone to slide through.

Drape the pastry over the top of the filling, poking the shin bone through the cross. Press the edges onto the rim of the tray. Trim away the excess pastry and brush the pie lid with egg wash. Bake in the oven for 30 minutes until the pastry is golden brown.

Serve the pie hot from the oven. I like to serve a bowl of good homemade chips on the side.

Chilli beef and butter bean pie

I often batch-cook at home and always have some chilli in the freezer. To keep it interesting, rather than just pile it onto rice, I started making chilli pie and serving it with creamy mash. It's now become a favourite family supper. If you possibly can, buy good-quality mince with a reasonable fat content from a butcher – the end result will be much tastier.

Serves 4

250g rough puff (page 28) or
   shortcrust pastry (page 16)
Flour, to dust
Egg wash (beaten egg)

For the filling
1 tbsp sunflower oil
250g minced beef
   (at least 20% fat)
2 onions, diced
4 garlic cloves, chopped
2 red peppers, cored, deseeded
   and sliced
2 medium-heat red chillies,
   deseeded and finely chopped
2 tbsp ground cumin
1 tbsp paprika
400g tin chopped tomatoes
2 tbsp soy sauce
200ml beef stock
2 x 400g tins butter beans,
   drained and rinsed
1 tbsp tomato purée
Sea salt and freshly cracked
   black pepper

Preheat the oven to 210°C/190°C Fan/Gas 6½.

For the filling, place a saucepan over a high heat and add the sunflower oil. Once hot, add the minced beef and stir, breaking it up so it doesn't clump together.

Once the meat is browned, add the onions, garlic, red peppers and chillies and cook for 10–15 minutes until the veg are softened. Add the cumin and paprika and cook for 2–3 minutes, then add the chopped tomatoes, soy sauce and stock.

Lower the heat and cook at a low simmer for at least 1 hour, adding a little water if the mixture seems likely to stick. Taste to check if the mince is tender; if it's not, continue to simmer.

Once the mince is tender, add the butter beans and tomato purée, then taste and season accordingly. Transfer the mixture to a deep pie dish or cast-iron pan, about 20cm in diameter and 12cm deep. Leave to cool.

Roll out the pastry on a lightly floured surface until it is large enough to cover the pie dish generously and about 5mm thick.

Drape the pastry over the filling and press the edges onto the rim of the dish. Trim away the excess pastry. Brush the pie lid with egg wash and pierce it in a couple of places to allow steam to escape. Bake in the oven for 30 minutes until the pastry is golden brown. Serve hot from the oven.

Chicken balti pie

Growing up in the Midlands, I've eaten many chicken curry pies, of varying quality. Using a balti recipe takes a curry pie to another level, with the peppers and tomatoes added late on lending freshness to the rich spicing. I wasn't sure how this pie would go down in Devon but when I cooked it for the staff at River Cottage they devoured it in no time!

Serves 4–6

500g rough puff (page 28) or
   shortcrust pastry (page 16)
Flour, to dust
Egg wash (beaten egg)

For the filling
4 large organic or free-range
   chicken legs (drumsticks and
   thighs), or 500g leftover
   roast chicken
4–5 tbsp light rapeseed oil
2 onions, finely sliced
50g fresh ginger, finely grated
6 garlic cloves, finely chopped
2 tsp ground cumin
1 tsp ground coriander
1 tsp ground turmeric
1 tsp ground cardamom
1 tsp nigella seeds
3 tbsp medium-heat curry powder
400g carton passata
400ml chicken stock
2 red peppers, cored, deseeded
   and cut into 2.5cm cubes
4 tomatoes, quartered
1 tbsp tomato purée
A bunch of coriander, leaves
   picked and roughly chopped
Sea salt and freshly cracked
   black pepper

Preheat the oven to 180°C/160°C Fan/Gas 4.

For the filling, put the chicken legs (if using) into a deep roasting tin, about 25 x 20cm, season well and trickle over 1 tbsp rapeseed oil. Cook in the oven for 1 hour.

Meanwhile, heat 3 tbsp rapeseed oil in a large saucepan over a low heat. Add the onions, ginger and garlic and cook for 45 minutes until soft and light brown.

Add all of the spices to the pan, stir and cook, stirring, for 3–4 minutes; don't be tempted to turn up the heat as the spices will burn; if the mixture is dry when the spices go in, add a little extra oil. Add the passata and stock and simmer gently for at least 20 minutes, stirring regularly.

Once the chicken is cooked, remove from the oven and leave until cool enough to handle. Pick the meat from the bones, finely dicing any skin; keep any juices in the roasting tin. Turn the oven up to 220°C/200°C Fan/Gas 7.

Add all the chicken and any juices to the spicy onion mix, with the peppers, tomatoes and tomato purée. Cook for 15 minutes. Stir in the coriander, then taste and season accordingly. Tip back into the roasting tin; leave to cool.

Roll out the pastry on a lightly floured surface until large enough to cover the roasting tin generously, and 5mm thick. Drape the pastry over the filling and press the edges onto the sides of the tin; trim away the excess.. Brush the pie lid with egg wash and make 4 slits in it. Bake for 20–25 minutes until the pastry is golden.

Steak, kidney and heart pudding

An absolute classic, steak and kidney pudding has been gracing tables for ages. Traditionally, the meat is added raw to the pastry casing but I prefer to precook the filling, so I can get the seasoning spot on. This also gives you a much saucier pudding. I've added heart to give another texture to the pudding, but you can use extra beef and kidney instead if you prefer.

Serves 4

For the filling
3 tbsp beef dripping, lard or
   rapeseed oil
400g beef chuck
2 pig's kidneys, trimmed and
   cut into 2cm pieces
2 pig's hearts, trimmed and
   cut into 2cm pieces
3 onions, sliced
4 garlic cloves, finely chopped
2 carrots, finely diced
4 sprigs of thyme
175ml full-bodied red wine
1 tbsp English mustard
2 tbsp Worcestershire sauce
1 tbsp tamari or soy sauce
1 tbsp miso (optional)
1 litre good-quality beef stock
About 1 tbsp cornflour, mixed to
   a paste with a little cold water

For the pastry
350g freshly made suet pastry
   (page 40)
Butter, to grease
Flour, to dust
Egg wash (optional)

To serve
Gravy (page 230)

Place a large saucepan over a high heat and add the fat/oil. When smoking hot, add the beef, kidney and heart and fry, stirring, until dark brown on all sides.

Lower the heat under the pan slightly. Add the onions, garlic, carrots and thyme to the pan and cook for around 7–10 minutes until the veg are golden brown. Add the wine, scraping up any tasty bits with a wooden spoon. Add the mustard, Worcestershire sauce, tamari or soy, miso, if using, and stock.

Bring to a simmer and lower the heat so the liquid is barely bubbling. Cook for 2 hours until the beef is soft but not falling apart. Trickle in the cornflour paste, stirring, until the sauce thickens (you may not need it all). Simmer for 1 minute then pick out the thyme. Taste and season well.

Grease and flour a 1 litre pudding basin. Following the instructions on page 43, line the basin with two-thirds of the suet pastry. Spoon in the filling, cover with the remaining pastry and seal the pastry edges.

Cover the basin with a pleated sheet of foil, securing it with string under the rim. Stand the basin on a small plate or trivet in a large, deep pan and pour in enough boiling water to come halfway up its sides. Put the lid on the pan and bring to a simmer over a medium heat. Steam the pud for 1 hour, topping up the boiling water as necessary.

Lift out the basin and remove the foil. Loosen the sides of the pudding with a knife, then invert onto a warmed plate. Serve with gravy, greens and new potatoes.

Spicy pork meatball, tomato and olive pie

Who doesn't love a meatball? These spicy little numbers are delicious and encasing them in pastry ensures they stay super-moist during the cooking process. Their tasty juices ooze into the tomato and olive sauce, giving it a wonderful flavour. Use good-quality butcher's mince that has a fair amount of fat – minced pork shoulder would be ideal.

Serves 6

500g rough puff pastry (page 28)
Flour, to dust
Egg wash (beaten egg)
A small handful of fennel seeds

For the meatballs
750g fatty pork mince
75g wholemeal breadcrumbs
5 garlic cloves, finely chopped
2 medium-heat chillies, deseeded
  and finely chopped
2 tsp paprika
1 tbsp English mustard
100g sun-dried tomatoes,
  finely chopped
A small bunch of oregano, leaves
  picked and chopped
3 spring onions, trimmed and
  finely chopped
Sea salt and freshly cracked
  black pepper

For the sauce
3 tbsp extra virgin olive oil
2 small onions, chopped
400g tin chopped tomatoes
150g green kalamata olives,
  pitted and sliced
200g cherry tomatoes
200g baby leaf spinach

To make the meatballs, mix all the ingredients together in a bowl, seasoning generously with salt and pepper. Shape the mixture into 3cm balls and set aside.

Preheat the oven to 210°C/190°C Fan/Gas 6½.

To make the sauce, heat the olive oil in a saucepan over a medium heat. Add the onions and cook for 10–15 minutes until softened. Add the tinned tomatoes and sliced olives and cook for a further 10–15 minutes until the sauce starts to thicken. Toss in the cherry tomatoes. Now add the spinach, a handful at a time, so it wilts down. Taste the sauce and season accordingly.

Meanwhile, spread the meatballs out in a deep roasting tray, about 25 x 20cm, and cook in the oven for about 10 minutes until they take on a little colour. Pour the sauce over the meatballs and return to the oven for another 10 minutes. Remove and set aside to cool.

Roll out the pastry on a lightly floured surface until large enough to cover the roasting tray generously, and about 5mm thick.

Drape the pastry over the filling and gently press the edges onto the sides of the tray; trim away the excess pastry. Pierce the pie lid in a few places, brush with egg wash and sprinkle with fennel seeds. Bake in the oven for 25–30 minutes until the pastry is golden brown.

Serve the pie hot from the oven – I find buttered gnocchi works well on the side.

Moroccan lamb shank pie

This ingredients list is lengthy but once the lamb is marinated, the rest is simple. The result is super-soft lamb in a spicy sauce with a hint of saffron. For visual effect, I leave some of the shanks whole with the bones poking through the pastry but you can take all the meat off the bone if you prefer.

Serves 6–8

500g rough puff pastry (page 28)
Flour, to dust
Egg wash (beaten egg)

For the filling
2 tsp ground cinnamon
2 tsp paprika
2 tsp ground coriander
2 tsp ground turmeric
2 tsp ground cardamom
1 tsp chilli powder, or more to taste
1 tsp saffron strands
6 lamb shanks
3 tbsp sunflower oil
3 onions, diced
4 garlic cloves, finely chopped
50g fresh ginger, finely chopped
Grated zest and juice of 2 limes
1 preserved lemon, peel only,
    finely chopped
2 x 400g tins chopped tomatoes
2 tbsp honey
300g dried apricots (unsulphured),
    chopped
1 litre lamb or chicken stock
A small bunch of coriander, leaves
    picked and roughly chopped
A small bunch of mint, leaves
    picked and roughly chopped
Sea salt and freshly cracked
    black pepper

For the filling, combine all the spices in a bowl. Put the lamb shanks into a large, deep roasting tray and rub with the spice mix, making sure every nook and cranny is coated. Leave to marinate in a cool place for at least 3 hours, preferably overnight.

Preheat the oven to 180°C/160°C Fan/Gas 4.

Place a large saucepan over a medium heat and add the oil, then the onions, garlic and ginger. Cook for 10 minutes or until the onions soften. Stir through the lime zest, preserved lemon, tomatoes, honey and dried apricots and bring to a simmer. Add the stock, taste and season well.

Pour the sauce over the lamb shanks and cover the tray with foil, sealing it under the rim. Transfer to the oven and cook for 4–5 hours, until the meat is very soft and tender.

Take out 3 lamb shanks and strip the meat from their bones. Tear it into bite-sized pieces and add back to the sauce with the herbs and lime juice. Stir gently so as not to pull the meat from the other shanks. Taste and add more seasoning if necessary. Allow to cool.

Roll out the pastry on a lightly floured surface until about 5mm thick and large enough to generously cover a large, deep pie dish, about 30 x 20cm and 8cm deep.

Stand the 3 lamb shanks up in your pie dish. Drape the pastry over the filling, pushing the bones through it. Brush the pie lid with egg wash and bake for 35 minutes until the pastry is golden brown. Serve hot from the oven, ideally with herby, lemony tabbouleh on the side.

Venison, celeriac, mushroom and juniper pie

Marinating the meat overnight is key here to muddle all the flavourings and mellow the stronger flavour of juniper. Once cooked, the rich flavour of the venison is levelled by the earthy celeriac and mushrooms, which give it a real taste of the forest. Source wild venison if you can: the wild population has to be controlled, so we might as well eat it rather than plump for farmed meat.

Serves 4

350g shortcrust pastry (page 16)
Flour, to dust
Egg wash (beaten egg)

For the filling
400g venison haunch, cut into 2cm dice
400g celeriac, cut into 1cm dice
1 tsp pink peppercorns, crushed (optional)
1 sprig of rosemary, roughly torn
200ml full-bodied red wine
5 juniper berries, crushed using a pestle and mortar
2 tbsp sunflower oil
2 onions, diced
3 garlic cloves, finely chopped
200g chestnut mushrooms, finely sliced
500ml game stock (or use good beef stock)
About 2 tbsp cornflour, mixed to a paste with a little cold water
Sea salt and freshly cracked black pepper

For the filling, put the venison into a large bowl with the celeriac, pink peppercorns if using, rosemary, wine and crushed juniper berries. Stir well, cover and leave the meat to marinate in the fridge overnight.

To cook the filling, heat the sunflower oil in a medium saucepan over a medium heat. Add the onions, garlic and mushrooms and cook for 10–15 minutes until softened.

Add the marinated venison and celeriac mix, including the flavourings and liquor. Pour in the stock and bring to a low simmer. Cook gently for about 1 hour until the meat is beautifully tender.

Preheat the oven to 180°C/160°C Fan/Gas 4. Trickle the cornflour paste into the venison mixture, stirring as you do so, until the sauce thickens (you may not need it all). Taste and season accordingly. Tip the filling into a deep pie dish, about 25cm in diameter. Leave to cool.

Roll out the pastry on a lightly floured surface until large enough to cover the pie dish generously, and 5mm thick. Drape the pastry over the filling and press the edges onto the rim of the dish. Trim away the excess pastry and crimp the edges. Cut leaves from the pastry trimmings.

Pierce the pie lid in a couple of places to allow steam to escape and brush the pastry with egg wash. Position the pastry leaves and brush these with egg wash. Bake in the oven for 25–30 minutes until the pastry is golden brown. Serve the pie hot from the oven, with root veg mash.

Creamy fish pie

There are a few pies that don't involve some kind of pastry and this is one of them. Topped with silky mash and a good smothering of cheese instead, it is delicious. You don't need to stress about the kind of fish you use as long as it is sustainably caught and there's a bit of smoked fish in there. If buying a fish pie mix, make sure you find out what's in it; often these include salmon, which is off our menu for ethical reasons.

Serves 6–8

For the topping
1kg floury potatoes, such as
   Maris Piper or King Edward,
   peeled and cut into 3cm pieces
100g butter, diced
150g mature Cheddar, grated
Sea salt and freshly cracked
   black pepper

For the filling
50g butter
50g plain flour
400ml fish stock
100ml white wine
150ml double cream
1kg sustainably caught mixed
   white fish, including at least
   250g smoked fish, diced
A generous bunch of flat-leaf
   parsley, leaves picked
   and chopped

For the topping, put the potatoes into a large saucepan, cover with cold water and add salt. Bring to the boil over a high heat then lower the heat and cook for about 20 minutes until the potatoes are completely soft. Drain in a colander and allow to steam-dry for a few minutes.

Tip the potatoes into a large bowl, add the butter and mash until smooth. Taste and season accordingly with salt and pepper. Set aside.

Preheat the oven to 220°C/200°C Fan/Gas 7.

For the filling, place a medium saucepan over a medium heat and add the butter. Once melted, add the flour, stir well and cook, stirring, for a minute. Now slowly add the stock, stirring all the time until you have a thick, smooth sauce. Add the white wine and cream, bring to a simmer and cook, stirring constantly, for 5 minutes.

Remove from the heat, add the fish and chopped parsley and stir to mix. Tip the filling into a deep pie dish, about 25 x 15cm and 12cm deep, and then top with the mash; I dollop it on to create peaks (to take on good colour) and troughs (to collect the melted cheese).

Sprinkle the cheese over the mash and then bake the pie in the oven for 15 20 minutes until the sauce is bubbling up around the sides and the cheese is golden brown.

Serve hot from the oven, with Savoy cabbage seasoned with plenty of black pepper.

Stargazy pie

Originating from the village of Mousehole in Cornwall, this is traditionally eaten on Tom Bawcock's Eve, a festival to celebrate Tom's heroic catch one day during a very stormy winter. There are differing stories explaining why the heads poke through the pastry but the most likely is to prove there was actual fish in the pie. In effect, it looks like the fish are leaping from the water to gaze at the stars!

Serves 4

500g rough puff pastry (page 28)
Flour, to dust
Egg wash (beaten egg)

For the filling
4 medium eggs, at room
   temperature
150g piece of streaky bacon,
   derinded and cut into 1cm cubes
50g unsalted butter
1 onion, finely chopped
1 leek, trimmed and finely chopped
2 garlic cloves, finely chopped
50g plain flour
500ml fish stock
100ml double cream
6 anchovy fillets, finely chopped
A small bunch of dill, leaves picked
   and finely chopped
A small bunch of flat-leaf parsley,
   leaves picked and finely chopped
8 MSC-certified Cornish sardines
   (or butterflied small mackerel
   for an easier eating experience)
Sea salt and freshly cracked
   black pepper

First prepare the filling. Bring a small pan of water to the boil and have a bowl of iced water ready. Gently lower the eggs into the water and cook for 7 minutes, then remove and immerse in the iced water to stop the cooking. Once cooled, lift out the boiled eggs, peel and roughly chop.

Place a saucepan over a medium heat, add the bacon and cook, stirring, until golden brown. Add the butter, then the onion, leek and garlic, and sweat for 5 minutes to soften. Stir in the flour and cook, stirring, for 1 minute. Now gradually add the stock, stirring to keep the mixture smooth. Simmer, stirring, for 5 minutes.

Preheat the oven to 200°C/180°C Fan/Gas 6. Add the cream, anchovies, herbs and chopped eggs to the sauce and stir gently to combine. Taste and season accordingly. Transfer the creamy filling mix to a deep pie dish, about 25cm in diameter and 12cm deep. Position the fish in the sauce with their heads poking up.

Roll out the pastry on a lightly floured surface until large enough to cover the pie dish generously, and about 5mm thick. Drape it over the filling then carefully cut a hole in the pastry above each fish and poke the head through. Press the edges of the pasty onto the rim of the dish and trim away the excess. Crimp the edges.

Brush the pastry with egg wash and bake the pie in the oven for 45–50 minutes until the pastry is deep golden brown. Serve at once, with greens and new potatoes.

Provençal seafood pie

This is a beautiful combination of fish and shellfish, flavoured with saffron and preserved lemon. It's a little like a bouillabaisse, with juicy fillets of fish to dish up with the shellfish and tomato sauce. I love the sweet potato and lemon topping – the slightly burnt bits of lemon are arguably the best bit.

Serves 4–6

For the topping
500g sweet potatoes, peeled
1 lemon, very thinly sliced,
    pips removed
2 tbsp olive oil
Sea salt and freshly cracked
    black pepper

For the filling
2 tbsp extra virgin olive oil
1 medium onion, diced
1 small fennel bulb, trimmed and
    finely chopped
2 garlic cloves, finely chopped
150ml dry white wine
400g tin chopped tomatoes
A few sprigs of thyme
A pinch of saffron strands
A small bunch of dill, leaves picked
    and finely chopped
300ml fish stock
250g mussels, cleaned
250g clams or cockles, cleaned
100g mixed white and brown
    crab meat
400–500g gurnard, red mullet
    or bream fillets, skinned and
    checked for pin-bones
400–500g hake fillets, skinned
    and checked for pin-bones

For the topping, finely slice the sweet potatoes and place in a bowl with the lemon slices and olive oil. Season well with salt and pepper, toss to mix and put to one side.

For the filling, heat the olive oil in a saucepan over a medium heat and add the onion, fennel and garlic. Sweat for 5 minutes to soften then pour in the wine. Let bubble for 1 minute then add the tomatoes, thyme, saffron, dill and half the stock. Bring to a simmer and cook, stirring often, for about 20 minutes until reduced and thickened.

Meanwhile, heat up a large saucepan over a high heat. When very hot, add the mussels and clams/cockles with the remaining 150ml stock. Cover with a tight-fitting lid and cook for 1 minute then give the pan a shake and cook for another 2 minutes. Shake and lift the lid. The shells should have opened; discard any that haven't. Scoop the molluscs into a bowl and allow to cool.

Pour the cooking liquor through a muslin-lined sieve into a bowl to remove any grit then add to the tomato sauce and set aside to cool. Pick the mussels and clams/cockles from their shells and add to the tomato sauce. Stir in the crab meat and season to taste.

Spread half of the shellfish sauce in a deep pie dish, about 25cm in diameter and 10cm deep. Season the fish fillets and arrange them in the dish. Cover with the remaining sauce and layer the sweet potato and lemon slices on top.

Bake in the oven for 35–45 minutes until the fish fillets are cooked through. Serve hot from the oven, with a crunchy salad on the side.

Spicy squash, onion and bean pie

Squash is such a versatile veg and one of our favourites at River Cottage. It is robust enough to take plenty of spice. For this pie filling, the spice elevates squash beautifully, and using coconut milk rather than cream gives a lighter, fruitier finish. I'm not too fussy about the beans I use, but black beans do have their own unique richness which sits well in this dish.

Serves 4

500g shortcrust pastry (page 16)
Flour, to dust
Egg wash (beaten egg)

For the filling
3 onions, quartered
4 garlic cloves, finely chopped
3 tbsp cold-pressed rapeseed oil
2 medium-heat red chillies,
    deseeded and finely chopped
3 sprigs of thyme
1kg squash, such as butternut or
    Crown Prince, peeled and cut
    into 2cm cubes
1 tbsp medium-heat curry powder
400ml coconut milk
A small bunch of coriander, leaves
    picked and roughly chopped
400g tin kidney beans, drained
400g tin black beans, drained
Sea salt and freshly cracked
    black pepper

Preheat the oven to 200°C/180°C Fan/Gas 6.

Put the onions and garlic into a deep pie dish, about 25cm in diameter and 5cm deep, trickle over the rapeseed oil and toss to coat. Cook in the oven for 15 minutes, stirring halfway through.

Remove the dish and add the chillies, thyme and squash. Season well and give everything a good stir. Return to the oven for 15 minutes until the squash just starts to soften.

Take out the dish again and add the curry powder, coconut milk, chopped coriander and tinned beans. Mix well then taste and adjust the seasoning, if necessary. Return to the oven for 15–20 minutes, until the sauce is thick and bubbling, giving it a good stir halfway through. Remove from the oven and set aside to cool down.

Roll out the pastry on a lightly floured surface until large enough to cover the pie dish generously, and about 5mm thick. Drape the pastry over the filling and press the edges onto the rim of the dish. Trim away the excess pastry and crimp the edges. Cut decorations from the trimmings if you like.

Pierce the pie lid in a couple of places and brush the pastry with egg wash. Position any pastry decorations and brush these with egg wash too. Bake in the oven for 25–30 minutes until the pastry is golden brown.

Serve hot from the oven, with a crisp green veg, such as mangetout or sugar snaps.

5
RAISED PIES

What is more British than a pork pie? Deep golden-brown pastry encasing highly seasoned succulent pork in a rich peppery jelly – it's so inviting. This famous-of-all raised pie dates back to the Middle Ages when the purpose of the pastry was to preserve the filling rather than to be eaten. Nowadays, of course, the pastry is as much a part of the pie as the meat.

Once found gracing the high tables of medieval kings and queens, the pork pie has somewhat lost its way and is now more often associated with cheap, inferior shop-bought imitations to stick in lunch boxes or eat on the go. If these are all you have ever eaten, please make the Classic River Cottage pork pie overleaf; it will change your perception forever! I like to make a big pie, as it looks so majestic, but the recipe works just as well for individual small pies.

In addition to the classic round raised pies, I explore the long, loaf-shaped pâté en croûte in this chapter. I've also given a few recipes for a few more straightforward shapes, so if time is tight you can still get some lovely individual raised pies in the oven. Fillings vary from traditional to funky, including my meaty favourite, Gala pie (on page 138), and first-choice veggie option, spiced carrot and fennel on page 157. So, whatever takes your fancy, give it a try – you'll be surprised how satisfying it is to make one of these historical wonders.

Classic River Cottage pork pie

This recipe first appeared in the *River Cottage Meat Book* and quite frankly I've never found a better one, so the credit here lies with Hugh. The seasoning of peppers and mace are spot on; the only thing which I've added in is an exact amount of salt, to ensure your seasoning will be just right every time. I always make one big pie and serve it sliced, but you can make smaller pies, which are slightly easier to transport for picnics or packed lunches, if you like.

Serves 8

1kg hot water crust pastry
   (page 33)
Flour, to dust
Egg wash (beaten egg)

For the filling
1kg pork shoulder, minced
250g pork belly, minced
   (or fatty sausage meat)
250g salt pork, pancetta or streaky
   bacon, finely chopped
12 sage leaves, finely chopped
2 sprigs of thyme, leaves picked
   and chopped
20g salt
2 tsp coarsely ground black pepper
2 tsp ground white pepper
½ tsp ground mace
A good pinch of cayenne pepper

For the jelly
400ml good-quality pork stock
8 sheets of bronze leaf gelatine

Preheat the oven to 200°C/180°C Fan/Gas 6.

To prepare the filling, put all the meats into a large bowl with the herbs, salt and all the other seasonings. Mix well until thoroughly combined.

To assemble the pie, cut off a generous quarter of the pastry and set aside; this will be your lid. On a lightly floured surface, roll out the bigger piece of pastry to a large round, about 1cm thick and 35cm in diameter.

Drape the pastry over a 20cm springform cake tin and use to line the tin (as detailed on page 34), pressing the pastry into the sides and flattening any overlap with your fingers. It should come 6–8cm up the sides of the tin.

Fill the pastry case with the seasoned pork mixture. Trim the pastry roughly, leaving a little overhang. Roll out the reserved piece of pastry to a 20cm round (the diameter of the tin) and about 1cm thick.

Brush the edges of the lining pastry lightly with egg wash and lay the pastry lid on top of the pie. Press the edges together to seal and trim away the excess pastry. Crimp the edges (see page 34). Brush the pie lid generously with egg wash and cut a 1cm hole in the centre.

Bake in the oven for 30 minutes, then lower the setting to 190°C/170°C Fan/Gas 5 and bake for a further 1 hour.

continued overleaf

Remove from the oven, release the spring clip and lift off the side of the tin. Brush the top and sides of the pastry well with egg wash and return to the oven for 15 minutes or until golden brown all over. A probe thermometer inserted into the centre of the pie should register 72°C. Remove from the oven and leave to cool for an hour or so.

For the jelly, heat the stock in a saucepan over a medium heat until it starts to steam, then add the gelatine leaves one by one, stirring constantly until fully melted. Remove from the heat and pour into a jug.

Using a funnel, pour the stock, little by little, into the pie through the hole in the pastry lid. Once full, allow the liquid to settle and repeat the process; keep doing this until you have got every last drop you can into the pie. Refrigerate for 5–6 hours to chill thoroughly. Remove the pie from the tin and cut into slices to serve.

Individual pork pies
Roll out the pastry to a 5mm thickness and cut out six 18cm rounds. Gather the pastry trimmings, re-roll and cut six 6cm rounds for the lids. Brush the edges of the larger pastry rounds with egg wash and place a couple of heaped spoonfuls of the filling in the centre.

Bring the pastry up around the sides of the filling and place the smaller pastry rounds on top. Press the edges together to seal all the way around and crimp them. Make a 1cm hole in the centre of each pie lid.

Place on a lined baking sheet and bake in the preheated oven at 190°C/170°C Fan/Gas 5 for 30 minutes. Remove from the oven and leave to cool for about 45 minutes. The cooled pies can be filled with jelly, as above.

Gala pie

This is a different take on a pork pie, with hard-boiled eggs running through the centre of the filling. Typically made in a terrine, it's stunning to look at and to eat – perfect to take pride of place on a Boxing Day buffet table. Or wrap up a good hunk to sustain you on a long walk. As ever, good-quality, reasonably fatty mince is key to the flavour. If you haven't got a terrine, a large loaf tin will do. (*Illustrated overleaf*)

Serves 10

1kg hot water crust pastry
　(page 33)
Butter, to grease
Flour, to dust
Egg wash (beaten egg)

For the filling
6 medium eggs (at room
　temperature)
500g pork shoulder, minced
125g pork belly, minced (or fatty
　sausage meat)
125g salt pork, pancetta or streaky
　bacon, finely chopped
1 boneless chicken breast, skinned
　and cut into 1cm dice
6 sage leaves, finely chopped
1 sprig of thyme, leaves picked
　and chopped
10g salt
1 tsp coarsely ground black pepper
1 tsp ground white pepper
½ tsp ground mace
A good pinch of cayenne pepper

For the jelly
200ml good-quality pork stock
4 sheets of bronze leaf gelatine

Preheat the oven to 200°C/180°C Fan/Gas 6.

Bring a medium saucepan of water to the boil and have a bowl of iced water ready. Carefully lower the eggs into the water and cook for 7 minutes, stirring gently to keep the eggs moving (and help centre the yolk), then remove and immerse in the iced water to stop the cooking. Once cooled, lift the boiled eggs out, peel them and set aside.

To make the filling, put all of the meats into a large bowl with the herbs, salt and other seasonings. Mix well until thoroughly combined.

Grease a terrine or loaf tin, 32 x 12cm and 10cm deep, with butter and then dust with flour, ensuring the mould is well coated and shaking out any excess flour.

Take a quarter of the pastry and put to one side; this will be the lid. Roll out the large piece of pastry on a lightly floured surface to a large rectangle, 1cm thick. Drape this over the loaf tin and carefully push into the mould to line it fully, taking care not to break the pastry. Trim the pastry, leaving a little overhanging the top, and brush with egg wash.

Spoon half of the meat filling into the pastry-lined tin, spread evenly and press down firmly. Lay the boiled eggs down the centre, packing them together tightly. Cover with the remaining filling and press firmly, but not so hard that you break the eggs.

Roll out the reserved piece of pastry to a rectangle large enough to cover the top of the tin generously, and 1cm thick. Brush the edges of the lining pastry with a little egg wash and lay the pastry lid over the top of the pie. Press the edges together to seal and crimp them (see page 34); you can use any trim to make some decorative shapes.

Brush the pie lid well with egg wash and cut 3 holes, 1cm in diameter along the middle of the pastry. Position any pastry decorations on top and brush these with egg wash too.

Bake in the oven for 15 minutes and then lower the oven setting to 190°C/170°C Fan/Gas 5 and bake for a further 40–45 minutes until the meat is cooked. A probe thermometer inserted into the centre of the pie should register 72°C.

Remove the pie from the oven and set aside to cool for about an hour.

For the jelly, heat the stock in a saucepan over a medium heat until it starts to steam, then add the gelatine leaves one by one, stirring constantly until fully melted. Remove from the heat and pour into a jug.

Using a funnel, pour the stock, little by little, into the pie through the holes in the pastry lid. Once full, allow the liquid to settle and repeat the process; keep doing this until you are confident you have got every last drop you can into the pie. Refrigerate for 5–6 hours until thoroughly chilled.

Remove the pie from the tin and cut into slices to serve.

Ham, fig and pumpkin seed pâté en croûte

I usually make this a day or two ahead for Christmas Eve, when it's so useful to have lots of lovely food ready to go that you can just whip out for gatherings or impromptu guests. Figs always remind me of Christmas and they are a lovely inclusion here. I guarantee you, this recipe will leave everyone seriously impressed. (*Illustrated overleaf*)

Serves 8–10

1kg hot water crust pastry
    (page 33)
Butter, to grease
Flour, to dust
Egg wash (beaten egg)

For the ham hock
1 ham hock (about 800g)
A generous bunch of flat-leaf
    parsley, stalks separated, leaves
    finely chopped
1 carrot, diced
1 onion, diced
1 celery stick, roughly diced

For the filling
500g pork shoulder, minced
125g pork belly, minced (or fatty
    sausage meat)
125g salt pork, pancetta or streaky
    bacon, finely chopped
6 sage leaves, finely chopped
2 sprigs of rosemary, leaves picked
    and finely chopped
100g pumpkin seeds, toasted
10g salt
1 tsp coarsely ground black pepper
1 tsp ground white pepper
½ tsp ground mace
A good pinch of cayenne pepper

Preheat the oven to 200°C/180°C Fan/Gas 6.

Place the ham hock in a large pan of cold water and bring to the boil. Taste the water and, if it is too salty, discard and replace with fresh water (you can repeat this process a couple of times if necessary).

Once the water just has a light salty tang, add the parsley stalks, carrot, onion and celery and simmer for 3–4 hours until the meat is very tender and falling from the bone. Lift the ham hock out of the stock onto a board and leave to cool.

Once cooled, use your hands to break the ham into large chunks and set aside for assembling the pâté en croûte.

To make the filling, put all the pork meats into a large bowl with the herbs, pumpkin seeds, salt and all the other seasonings. Mix well until thoroughly combined.

Grease a terrine mould, 30 x 11cm and 8cm deep, with butter and then dust with flour, ensuring the mould is well coated and shaking out any excess flour.

Take a quarter of the pastry and put to one side; this will be the lid. Roll out the large piece of pastry on a lightly floured surface to a large rectangle, 1cm thick. Drape this over the terrine and carefully push into the mould to line it fully, taking care not to break the pastry.

Trim the pastry, leaving a little overhanging the top, and brush with egg wash.

To assemble
8 figs, trimmed

For the jelly
400ml ham stock (from cooking
   the hock)
8 sheets of bronze leaf gelatine

Spoon one-third of the meat filling into the pastry-lined terrine, spread evenly and press down firmly. Layer the ham chunks on top, packing them together tightly, then arrange the figs on top. Cover with the remaining meat filling and press firmly, ensuring the ham and figs are well surrounded and covered by meat.

Roll out the reserved piece of pastry to a rectangle large enough to cover the top of the terrine generously, and 1cm thick. Brush the edges of the lining pastry with a little egg wash and lay the pastry lid over the top of the pie. Press the edges together to seal and crimp them (see page 34).

Brush the pastry lid well with egg wash and cut 2 or 3 holes, 1cm in diameter, along the middle of the pastry.

Bake in the oven for 30 minutes then lower the oven setting to 190°C/170°C Fan/Gas 5 and bake for a further 40–45 minutes, until a probe thermometer inserted into the centre of the pâté en croûte registers 72°C. Remove from the oven and leave to cool for an hour.

For the jelly, heat the stock in a saucepan over a medium heat until it starts to steam, then add the gelatine leaves one by one, stirring constantly until fully melted. Remove from the heat and pour into a jug.

Using a funnel, gradually pour the jellied stock into the pâté en croûte through the holes in the pastry lid. Once full, allow the liquid to settle and repeat the process; keep doing this until you are confident you have got every last drop you can into the pie. Refrigerate for 5–6 hours until thoroughly chilled.

Carefully remove the pie from the terrine and cut into slices to serve.

Smoked duck pâté en croûte

A combination of slow-cooked duck leg and rich smoked duck breast is something you don't often see in a raised pie but it is seriously good. Everyone I've served this up to has been blown away! It is definitely one to make for a special occasion, with plenty of pickles and chutneys on the side to counteract the richness.

Serves 10

1kg hot water crust pastry
　(page 33)
Butter, to grease
Flour, to dust
Egg wash (beaten egg)

For the filling
2 large organic or free-range
　duck legs
500g pork shoulder, minced
125g pork belly, minced (or fatty
　sausage meat)
125g salt pork, pancetta or streaky
　bacon, finely chopped
2 tsp ground star anise
Finely grated zest of 2 oranges
10g salt
1 tsp coarsely ground black pepper
1 tsp ground white pepper
½ tsp ground mace
A good pinch of cayenne pepper
2 smoked duck breasts, skinned
　and halved lengthways
Sea salt and freshly cracked
　black pepper

For the jelly
200ml good-quality pork stock
4 sheets of bronze leaf gelatine

Preheat the oven to 170°C/150°C Fan/Gas 3.

For the filling, put the duck legs into a roasting tray, season with salt and pepper and cook in the oven for 1½ hours until completely tender. Remove and leave until cool enough to handle.

Tear the duck meat from the bone and break it into shreds; finely chop the skin. Chill the pan juices so the fat settles on top of the juice. Spoon the duck fat off and save it for roasting potatoes. Add the cooking juices to the pork stock for the jelly.

Put the duck meat and skin into a large bowl and add all the remaining filling ingredients, except the smoked duck breasts. Mix thoroughly to combine.

Heat the oven to 200°C/180°C Fan/Gas 6. Grease a terrine mould, 30 x 11cm and 8cm deep, with butter and then dust with flour, ensuring the mould is well coated and shaking out any excess flour.

Take a quarter of the pastry and put to one side; this will be for the lid. Roll out the large piece of pastry on a lightly floured surface to a large rectangle, about 1cm thick.

Drape the sheet of pastry over the terrine and carefully push it into the mould to line it fully, taking care not to break the pastry. Trim the pastry, leaving a little overhanging the top and brush with egg wash.

continued overleaf

Spoon one-third of the meat filling into the pastry-lined terrine, spread evenly and press down firmly. Lay two smoked duck breast halves on top and press down. Cover with another third of the meat filling, then layer the other two duck breast halves on top. Cover with the remaining meat filling, pushing down firmly.

Roll out the reserved piece of pastry to a rectangle large enough to cover the top of the terrine generously, and 1cm thick. Brush the edges of the lining pastry with a little egg wash and lay the pastry lid over the top of the pie. Press the edges together to seal and crimp them (see page 34).

Brush the pastry lid well with egg wash and cut 2 or 3 holes, 1cm in diameter, along the middle of the pastry.

Bake in the oven for 30 minutes then lower the oven setting to 190°C/170°C Fan/Gas 5 and bake for a further 45 minutes or until a probe thermometer inserted into the centre of the pâté en croûte registers 72°C. Remove from the oven and leave to cool for an hour.

For the jelly, heat the stock in a saucepan over a medium heat until it starts to steam, then add the gelatine leaves one by one, stirring constantly until fully melted. Remove from the heat and pour into a jug.

Using a funnel, pour the jellied stock, little by little, into the pâté en croûte through the holes in the pastry lid. Once full, allow the liquid to settle and repeat the process; keep doing this until you are confident you have got every last drop you can into the pie. Refrigerate for 5–6 hours until thoroughly chilled.

Carefully remove the pie from the terrine and cut into slices to serve.

Game pie

This is one of the classic raised pies. Choosing which game to put into your pie is important. Most game birds, especially pheasant and partridge, are raised in cramped sheds, akin to the sheds used for intensive poultry farming, until they reach a certain age when they are released to be shot en masse at organised shoots. For me, this makes these game birds no better ethically than the lowest standard of raising poultry that is legal in the UK. So, for this pie, I choose a mix of wild pigeon, venison and wild rabbit. A lot of the rabbit in this country is cage-reared in France, so do check the source of that too. As game is notoriously lean, you need some fatty pork mixed through the filling. (*Illustrated overleaf*)

Serves 8–10

1kg hot water crust pastry
  (page 33)
Flour, to dust
Egg wash (beaten egg)

For the filling
500g mixed game meat (wood
  pigeon, wild venison haunch
  and wild rabbit), diced
500g pork shoulder, minced
125g pork belly, minced (or fatty
  sausage meat)
125g salt pork, pancetta or streaky
  bacon, finely chopped
6 sage leaves, finely chopped
1 sprig of thyme, leaves picked
  and chopped
Finely grated zest of 2 oranges
20g salt
1 tsp coarsely ground black pepper
1 tbsp ground juniper berries
1 tbsp ground pink peppercorns
1 tsp ground white pepper
½ tsp ground mace
A good pinch of cayenne pepper

Preheat the oven to 200°C/180°C Fan/Gas 6.

To make the filling, put all the meats into a large bowl with the herbs, orange zest, salt and all the other seasonings. Mix well until thoroughly combined.

To assemble the pie, cut off a generous quarter of the pastry and set aside; this will be your lid. On a lightly floured surface, roll out the bigger piece of pastry to a large round, about 1cm thick and 35cm in diameter.

Drape the pastry over a 20cm springform cake tin and use to line the tin (as detailed on page 34), pressing the pastry into the sides and flattening any overlap with your fingers. It should come up the sides of the tin and overlap by at least 1cm.

Fill the pastry case with the seasoned game mixture. Trim the pastry roughly, leaving a little overhang. You can use the trimmings to cut decorations if you like. Roll out the reserved piece of pastry to a 20cm round (the diameter of the tin) and about 1cm thick.

Brush the edges of the lining pastry with a little egg wash, and lay the pastry lid on top of the pie. Press the edges together to seal and crimp them (see page 34). Cut a hole, 1cm in diameter, in the centre.

For the jelly
400ml game stock (or use good-
    quality pork stock)
8 sheets of bronze leaf gelatine

Position any pastry decorations on top of the pie and brush these with egg wash too.

Place the pie in the oven and bake for 30 minutes, then lower the oven setting to 190°C/170°C Fan/Gas 5 and bake for a further 1 hour.

Remove from the oven, release the spring clip and lift off the side of the tin. Brush the top and sides of the pastry well with egg wash and return to the oven for about 10 minutes until golden brown all over. A probe thermometer inserted into the centre of the pie should register 72°C.

Remove the pie from the oven and set aside to cool for about an hour.

For the jelly, heat the stock in a saucepan over a medium heat until it starts to steam, then add the gelatine leaves one by one, stirring constantly until fully melted. Remove from the heat and pour into a jug.

Using a funnel, pour the jellied stock, little by little, into the pie through the hole in the pastry lid. Once full, allow the liquid to settle and repeat the process; keep doing this until you are confident you have got every last drop you can into the pie. Refrigerate for 5–6 hours until thoroughly chilled.

Remove the pie from the tin and cut into slices to serve. I like to serve a pot of English mustard and some pickled veg on the side.

Sweet potato, greens and feta pies

This isn't a combination of ingredients you would expect to find in a traditionally British raised pie but the salty feta and olives cut through the sweet potato perfectly and it works a treat. It is always fun to make individual pies and watch people's reaction as they bite into something they aren't expecting!

Makes 6

1kg vegetarian hot water crust
   pastry (page 33)
Flour, to dust
Egg wash (beaten egg)

For the filling
1kg sweet potatoes, peeled and
   cut into 2cm cubes
1 small red onion, diced
2 garlic cloves, chopped
3 tbsp extra virgin olive oil
200g spring greens or kale, tough
   stalks removed, finely chopped
150g kalamata olives, pitted
   and halved
250g feta, cut into 1cm cubes
A small bunch of oregano, leaves
   picked and chopped
Sea salt and freshly cracked
   black pepper

Preheat the oven to 210°C/190°C Fan/Gas 6½.

For the filling, put the sweet potatoes, onion and garlic on a baking tray, trickle over the olive oil and toss to coat. Place in the oven and cook for 15 minutes until the potatoes start to soften.

Take out the tray, add the greens and stir through the potatoes. Return to the oven for 15 minutes, stirring halfway through. Remove from the oven and stir through the olives, feta and chopped oregano, then taste and season accordingly. Bash together to bind the mixture. Set aside to cool.

Line a baking sheet with baking paper. Roll out the pastry on a lightly floured surface to about a 5mm thickness and cut six 18cm rounds. Gather the pastry trimmings, re-roll and cut six 6cm rounds for the lids.

Brush the edges of the larger pastry rounds with egg wash. Pile a couple of heaped spoonfuls of filling into the centre of one of these rounds. Bring the pastry up around the filling and place one of the smaller circles on top. Press the pastry edges together, sealing the lid to the sides all the way around, then crimp them. Repeat with the rest of the filling and pastry.

Brush the pie lids with egg wash and cut a 1cm hole in the centre of each then place the pies on the lined baking sheet. Bake in the oven for 30 minutes or until deep golden brown. Serve hot or at room temperature.

Spiced carrot and fennel raised pie

This is a great pie to make for any celebration, especially one that includes vegetarians, and it proves that not every raised pie has to be filled with meat. The intriguing sweet spiced filling has a ring of slow-roasted carrots nestling in the centre of each slice. It's certainly a lovely thing to eat. Carrageenan is a natural thickening and emulsifying ingredient, extracted from seaweed.

Serves 8-10

1kg vegetarian hot water crust
   pastry (page 33)
Butter, to grease
Flour, to dust
Egg wash (beaten egg)

For the filling
1kg carrots
2 tbsp cold-pressed rapeseed oil
3 tbsp sunflower oil
2 onions, diced
3 garlic cloves, chopped
1 fennel bulb, trimmed and
   chopped
2 tsp fennel seeds
1 tsp coriander seeds
2 tsp ground cumin
100g ground almonds
A small bunch of flat-leaf parsley,
   leaves picked and finely chopped
1 tsp carrageenan powder
200ml veg stock
Sea salt and freshly cracked
   black pepper

Preheat the oven to 180°C/160°C Fan/Gas 4.

For the filling, trim the carrots, removing the pointy ends and trimming the wider ends so you have similar-width pieces; dice the carrot trim.

Place the thick carrot pieces in a roasting tray with the rapeseed oil and a splash of water. Season with salt and pepper and toss well. Cover with foil and cook in the oven for 1–1½ hours until the carrots are tender.

Place a saucepan over a medium heat and add the sunflower oil. Toss in the onions, garlic, diced carrot trim and fennel and cook, stirring regularly, for 15–20 minutes until all the veg are softened. Add the spice seeds and ground cumin and cook, stirring, for a few minutes.

Remove the pan from the heat and let the veg cool slightly then transfer to a food processor and pulse to a rough-textured mixture. Add the ground almonds, chopped parsley, carrageenan powder and veg stock and pulse briefly until just combined. Taste and season accordingly with salt and pepper.

Turn the oven up to 200°C/180°C Fan/Gas 6. Grease a terrine mould, 30 x 11cm and 8cm deep, with butter and then dust with flour, ensuring the mould is well coated and shaking out any excess flour.

Set aside a quarter of the pastry for the pie lid.

continued overleaf

Roll out the bigger piece of pastry on a lightly floured surface to a large rectangle, 1cm thick. Drape the sheet of pastry over the terrine and carefully push it into the mould to line it fully, taking care not to break the pastry. Trim the pastry, leaving a little overhanging the top.

Re-roll the pastry trimmings and cut decorations to finish the pie if you like.

Spoon one-third of the vegetable mixture into the pastry-lined terrine, spread evenly and press down firmly. Lay the whole roasted carrot pieces on top, packing them together tightly and pushing them down into the mix so there is a little filling in between them but no gaps. Cover with the remaining veg mixture, making sure the carrots are totally covered, and press down firmly.

Roll out the reserved piece of pastry to a rectangle large enough to cover the top of the terrine generously, and 1cm thick. Brush the edges of the lining pastry with a little egg wash and lay the pastry lid over the top of the pie. Press the edges together to seal and crimp them (see page 34).

Brush the pie lid well with egg wash and make a few slits along the pastry. Position any pastry decorations and brush these with egg wash too. Bake in the oven for 30 minutes, then lower the oven setting to 190°C/170°C Fan/Gas 5 and bake for a further 30 minutes.

Remove from the oven and leave to cool for about an hour, then refrigerate for 5–6 hours to chill thoroughly.

Remove the pie from the tin and cut into slices to serve.

Individual five-root pies

The filling for these pies can be served up as a dinner in its own right, but encasing it in crisp hot water crust pastry just makes it better. I like to bake individual pies that you can just pick up and munch away on.

Makes 8

1kg vegetarian hot water crust
    pastry (page 33)
Flour, to dust
Egg wash (beaten egg)

For the filling
500ml double cream
4 garlic cloves, bashed
5 sprigs of thyme
2 large floury potatoes, such as
    Maris Piper or King Edward
2 parsnips
1 swede, halved
3 carrots
1 celeriac
Sea salt and freshly cracked
    black pepper

Preheat the oven to 190°C/170°C Fan/Gas 5. Line a roasting tray, 38 x 25cm and 5cm deep, with baking paper.

For the filling, pour the cream into a saucepan, add the garlic and thyme and heat gently to infuse. As it comes to a simmer, season generously and take off the heat.

Peel and finely slice all of the veg and place in a large bowl. Strain the infused milk through a sieve onto the veg then tumble together. Pack the mixture into the lined tray and cover the surface with baking paper.

Cover the roasting tray with foil, sealing it under the rim, and cook in the oven for 1–1½ hours. To test, insert a knife into the centre; it should pass through easily. Allow to cool then lay a tray on top (one that just fits inside the tray), place 1kg weight(s) on top and refrigerate overnight.

When you're ready to assemble the pies, preheat the oven to 210°C/190°C Fan/Gas 6½ and line a baking sheet with baking paper. Remove the vegetable terrine from the fridge, turn out onto a board and cut into 8 squares.

Roll out the pastry on a lightly floured surface to a large rectangle, 60 x 30cm and 5mm thick. Cut this into eight 15cm squares and brush the edges with egg wash. Place a portion of the veg filling in the centre of a pastry square, bring the corners up over the filling and pinch together. Press the pastry edges together and crimp them to seal in the filling. Repeat with the remaining pastry and filling.

Brush the pies with egg wash and make 4 slits in the top of each one. Place on the lined baking sheet. Bake in the oven for 30 minutes until deep golden brown. Serve hot.

Slow-roast pepper and courgette pies

Hot water crust pastry is ideal to hold this flavourful mixture of summer veg. Keeping the veg chunky gives the filling texture, and roasting them all together slowly really intensifies the flavours. Including loads of herbs just adds to that wonderful taste of the Med.

Makes 8

1kg vegetarian hot water crust pastry (page 33)
Flour, to dust
Egg wash (beaten egg)

For the filling
2 small courgettes, cut into 1cm pieces
2 red or yellow peppers, cored, deseeded and cut into 2cm pieces
2 red onions, roughly chopped
3 tbsp extra virgin olive oil
400g tin green lentils, drained and rinsed
A small bunch of basil, leaves picked and torn
A small bunch of dill, leaves picked and roughly chopped
200g pumpkin seeds
2 tbsp tomato purée
Sea salt and freshly cracked black pepper

Preheat the oven to 170°C/150°C Fan/Gas 3.

For the filling, put the courgettes, peppers and onions into a roasting tray. Trickle over the olive oil, season and tumble together. Roast in the oven for 1 hour. Take out the tray and stir through the lentils and herbs. Set aside.

Turn the oven up to 210°C/190°C Fan/Gas 6½. Scatter the pumpkin seeds on a baking tray and toast in the oven for 6–8 minutes until they take on a little colour. Remove and let cool then blitz in a food processor to a rough, crumbly texture. Add to the roasted veg with the tomato purée and mix well. Taste and adjust the seasoning if necessary.

Line a baking sheet with baking paper. Roll out the pastry on a lightly floured surface to about a 5mm thickness and cut eight 18cm rounds. Gather the pastry trimmings, re-roll and cut eight 6cm rounds for the lids.

Brush the edges of the larger pastry rounds with egg wash. Pile a couple of heaped spoonfuls of filling in the centre of one of these rounds. Bring the pastry up around the filling and place one of the smaller circles on top. Press the pastry edges together, sealing the lid to the sides all the way around, then crimp them. Repeat with the rest of the filling and pastry.

Brush the pie lids with egg wash and make a few slits in the top of each. Place the pies on the lined baking sheet and bake in the oven for 30 minutes or until deep golden brown. Serve hot or at room temperature.

6
INDIVIDUAL PASTIES

The origins of the mighty pasty, which dates back to the thirteenth century, are shrouded in mystery. They seem to be firmly rooted in the Southwest, but there is still debate about which county owns it. Cornwall seems to have the edge though, with its Protected Geographical Indication, which designates that anything sold as a Cornish pasty has to be made in Cornwall. Of course, that doesn't mean that amazing pasties aren't produced all over the country.

One of the more interesting stories that surround the pasty is that it was originally crafted for miners and agricultural workers. The pasties could be eaten with dirty hands, as they were held by the thick pastry edge which was then discarded. They are certainly ideal for lunch on the run.

Other stories indicate pasties were intended to be eaten end to end, not least those that had a savoury lunch filling at one end and pudding at the other – a genius concept! In homage, I've given my recipe for Slow-roast pork and Bramley apple pasties on page 175, which are certainly fun to serve up.

The best classic pasties I've eaten have been in Devon and Cornwall – and my Cornish pasty recipe on page 166 is based on these. I swap half the butter for lard, which is the usual way for meat pasties and gives a slightly softer crust. Or you may prefer the more unusual chicken and chorizo pasties on page 173. And if you're looking to make veggie pasties, you'll find some great options here.

Classic Cornish pasties

The original pasty, dating as far back as the thirteenth century, is surrounded by folklore and its origin is still hotly contested throughout the Southwest. Without wanting to offend anyone, I've stuck with Cornish pasties, although for me that's more about the filling than the pasty's origin. It's a mixture of raw beef skirt, potatoes, onions and swede with lots of black pepper. You'll need to get skirt from the butcher's; other cuts simply don't work. I'll leave the arguments about who owns the pasty to those born and bred in the Southwest!

Makes 4 large pasties

750g shortcrust pastry (page 16),
    made with half butter, half lard
Flour, to dust
Egg wash (beaten egg)

For the filling
350g beef skirt, diced
1 medium onion, finely diced
2 medium floury potatoes, such
    as Maris Piper or King Edward,
    peeled and cut into 1cm cubes
150g swede, cut into 1cm cubes
Sea salt and freshly cracked
    black pepper

Preheat the oven to 220°C/200°C Fan/Gas 7 and line a baking tray with baking paper.

For the filling, mix the beef, onion, potatoes and swede together in a bowl and season liberally; a tradition pasty has lots of pepper so don't hold back!

Divide the pastry into 4 portions. Roll each out on a lightly floured surface to a rough circle, 3mm thick, and trim to a neat 22cm round, using an upturned plate or loose-bottomed cake/flan tin base as a guide.

Pile a quarter of the filling mixture onto one side of each pastry round, leaving a 3cm clear margin around the edge. Brush the pastry border with egg wash, then fold the other side of the pastry over the filling and bring the edges together. Press the pastry edges firmly to seal and crimp them with your thumb and forefinger. Brush the top of the pastry with egg wash.

Place the pasties on the lined baking tray and bake in the oven for 10 minutes, then lower the oven setting to 180°C/160°C Fan/Gas 4 and cook for another 45 minutes until golden brown.

Mince, potato and gravy pasties

Mince can make a very tasty and especially saucy filling for a pasty (don't be put off by shop-bought versions). You can't just pop it in raw though – it needs a long slow cook with flavourings beforehand to ensure it is tender and delicious. The gravy it makes is the highlight for me.

Makes 4 large pasties

750g shortcrust pastry (page 16),
    made with half butter, half lard
Flour, to dust
Egg wash (beaten egg)
4 sprigs of thyme

For the filling
2 tbsp sunflower oil
300g beef mince
2 onions, diced
3 garlic cloves, finely chopped
3 sprigs of thyme
2 tbsp tamari or soy sauce
500ml beef stock
500g floury potatoes, such as
    Maris Piper or King Edward,
    peeled and cut into 1cm cubes
About 2 tbsp cornflour, mixed to
    a paste with a little cold water
Sea salt and freshly cracked
    black pepper

For the filling, place a large saucepan over a high heat and add the sunflower oil, followed by the mince. Cook, stirring and breaking up the mince using the back of a wooden spoon, until it is a good golden-brown colour.

Add the onions with the garlic and thyme and cook for a further 5 minutes or until softened. Add the tamari or soy and stock. Stir well and bring to a simmer, then lower the heat and cook gently for 45 minutes. Add the potatoes and simmer for 15 minutes or until they are just softened. Pick out the thyme stalks.

Slowly trickle in the cornflour paste, stirring as you do so, until the sauce thickens (you may not need it all). Cook, stirring, for a couple of minutes then taste and season accordingly. Remove from the heat and leave to cool.

Preheat the oven to 220°C/200°C Fan/Gas 7. Line a baking tray with baking paper. Divide the pastry into 4 portions. Roll each out on a lightly floured surface to a rough circle, 3mm thick, and trim to a 22cm round, using an upturned plate or loose-bottomed cake/flan tin base as a guide.

Pile a quarter of the filling onto one side of each pastry round, leaving a 3cm border. Brush the border with egg wash, then fold the other side of the pastry over the filling and bring the edges together. Press the edges to seal and crimp them. Brush the top of the pastry with egg wash.

Place the pasties on the baking tray, sprinkle with salt and pepper and lay a thyme sprig on each. Bake for 10 minutes then lower the oven setting to 200°C/180°C Fan/Gas 6. Bake for another 15 minutes until golden brown.

Lamb tagine pasties

I'm a big fan of North African food so to me it makes complete sense to fill a pasty full of spicy, aromatic lamb tagine. At home, these only last a matter of minutes, so expect these pasties to be a big hit!

Makes 4 large pasties

750g shortcrust pastry (page 16), made with half butter, half lard
Flour, to dust
Egg wash (beaten egg)

For the lamb
400g diced lamb shoulder
2 tsp ground cinnamon
2 tsp paprika
2 tsp ground coriander
2 tsp ground turmeric
2 tsp ground cardamom
1 tsp chilli powder
1 tsp saffron strands

For the sauce
3 onions, diced
4 garlic cloves, finely chopped
50g fresh ginger, finely chopped
Grated zest and juice of 2 limes
1 preserved lemon, peel only, finely chopped
2 x 400g tins chopped tomatoes
2 tbsp honey
300g dried apricots (unsulphured), chopped
1 tbsp tomato purée
A small bunch of coriander, leaves picked and roughly chopped
A small bunch of mint, leaves picked and roughly chopped
Sea salt and freshly cracked black pepper

Put the lamb into a large bowl, sprinkle with all the spices and toss well to coat. Cover and leave to marinate in a cool spot for at least 3 hours, preferably overnight in the fridge.

Once marinated, transfer the spice-coated lamb to a large saucepan and add all of the sauce ingredients except the tomato purée and fresh herbs, seasoning lightly with salt and pepper. Bring to a simmer and cook gently for 1½–2 hours until the meat is tender. Add a little water if necessary during cooking to prevent sticking, but keep the sauce nice and thick.

Add the tomato purée and chopped herbs, then taste and adjust the seasoning. Set aside to cool.

Preheat the oven to 220°C/200°C Fan/Gas 7 and line a large baking tray with baking paper. Divide the pastry into 4 portions. Roll each portion out on a lightly floured surface to a rough circle, 3mm thick, and trim to a neat 22cm round, using an upturned plate or loose-bottomed cake/flan tin base as a guide.

Pile a quarter of the filling mixture in the centre of each pastry round, leaving a 3cm clear margin around the edge. Brush the pastry border with egg wash, then bring the opposite sides of the pastry up over the top of the filling so the edges meet. Press the pastry edges firmly to seal and crimp them with your thumb and forefinger. Brush the top of the pastry with egg wash.

Place the pasties on the lined baking tray and bake in the oven for 10 minutes, then lower the oven setting to 200°C/180°C Fan/Gas 6 and cook for another 15 minutes until golden brown.

Willow's chicken and chorizo pasties

These are my stepdaughter Willow's favourite pasties, inspired by those she buys from a little shop in Lyme Regis. The chorizo mix is delicious and can be used for far more than just popping into pasties.

Makes 4 large pasties

750g shortcrust pastry (page 16),
 made with half butter, half lard
Flour, to dust
Egg wash (beaten egg)

For the chorizo
250g fatty pork, coarsely minced
1 tsp smoked paprika
1 tsp sweet paprika
1 tsp fennel seeds, toasted
2 garlic cloves, finely chopped
A splash of red wine
A pinch of cayenne pepper
 (or more if you like it hot)
3g salt

For the filling
2 organic or free-range
 chicken thighs (bone in)
2 onions, sliced
2 large floury potatoes, such as
 Maris Piper or King Edward,
 peeled and cut into 1cm cubes
A small bunch of chives, finely
 chopped
A small bunch of oregano or basil,
 leaves picked and chopped
Sea salt and freshly cracked
 black pepper

First, make the chorizo: mix all the ingredients together in a large bowl. Cover and leave to stand in a cool place for at least 3 hours, preferably overnight in the fridge.

Preheat the oven to 180°C/160°C Fan/Gas 4. For the filling, put the chicken thighs into a roasting tray, season and roast for 1–1½ hours until very tender and falling from the bone. Transfer to a plate. Tip the tray juices into a jug.

Roll the chorizo into little balls and place in the (now empty) roasting tray with the onions. Trickle over some of the chicken juices. Cook in the oven for 20 minutes, stirring halfway through. Meanwhile, pick the chicken meat off the bones and tear into bite-sized pieces.

Add the potatoes, chicken and remaining juices to the tray. Return to the oven for 7–10 minutes until the potato is just cooked and the liquor is absorbed. Stir through the herbs, taste and adjust the seasoning. Allow to cool.

Preheat the oven to 220°C/200°C Fan/Gas 7. Line a baking tray with baking paper. Divide the pastry into 4 portions and roll each out to a rectangle, 25 x 20cm.

Pile a quarter of the filling onto one side of each pastry rectangle, leaving a 3cm clear border around the edge. Brush the pastry border with egg wash, then fold the other side of the pastry over the filling, bringing the edges together. Press the edges firmly to seal and brush the top of the pastry with egg wash. Sprinkle with pepper.

Lay the pasties on the baking tray. Bake for 10 minutes, then lower the oven setting to 200°C/180°C Fan/Gas 6 and cook for another 15 minutes until golden brown.

Slow-roast pork and Bramley apple pasties

Back in history, there are stories told of pasties being an entire meal – with savoury at one end and dessert at the other. It's such a wonderful idea that I really had to include a recipe in this chapter. And why not get age-old friends, pork and apple, to snuggle up together in a pasty? I use juicy slow-cooked pork shoulder for the filling, which yields some good crackling that I suggest you chop in (though I confess to eating a fair bit of it before it makes it to the chopping board). I like to make the pasties about two-thirds pork, one-third sweet Bramley apple, but at least one person in my house would like that ratio reversed.

Makes 4 large pasties

750g shortcrust pastry (page 16), made with half butter, half lard
Flour, to dust
Egg wash (beaten egg)

For the meat filling
1 onion, sliced
2 carrots, sliced
2 garlic cloves, bashed
500g piece of fatty pork shoulder
4 sage leaves, finely chopped
Sea salt and freshly cracked black pepper

For the apple filling
600g Bramley apples, peeled and cut into small pieces
50g demerara sugar
2 sprigs of thyme

For the glaze
20g demerara sugar
½ tsp ground mixed spice

Preheat the oven to 160°C/140°C Fan/Gas 3.

To prepare the meat filling, put the onion, carrots and garlic into a roasting dish. Season the pork skin with salt and sit the piece of meat on top of the vegetables. Pour enough water into the dish to give a 2.5cm depth. Cover the dish with foil and cook in the oven for 2½ hours.

Remove the foil and turn the oven up to 220°C/210°C Fan/Gas 7. Cook for a further 15–20 minutes until the pork skin crackles then remove and set aside.

Meanwhile, to prepare the apple filling, put the Bramley apples into a saucepan with the sugar, thyme and 2 tbsp water. Cook over a medium heat, stirring regularly for about 7–10 minutes, until the apples start to break down. Pick out the thyme stalks and allow to cool.

When the pork is cool enough to handle, lift it on to a board. Remove the crackling, finely chop it and set aside.

Tear the meat into small strands and place in a bowl. Break up the roasted onion, carrots and garlic and add to the bowl. Mix with the pork, adding enough of the roasting juices to soften the mixture, then stir through the chopped crackling and sage. Taste and season accordingly with salt and pepper.

continued overleaf

Line a baking tray with baking paper. Divide the pastry into 4 portions. Roll each out on a lightly floured surface to a rough circle, 3mm thick, and trim to a neat 22cm round, using an upturned plate or loose-bottomed cake/flan tin base as a guide.

Leaving a 3cm clear margin around the edge, pile a quarter of the meat filling mixture onto the top half of each pastry round, along the middle. Now pile a quarter of the apple filling onto the lower half of each pastry round, along the middle. Brush the pastry border with egg wash.

Bring the opposite sides of the pastry up over the top of the filling so the edges meet in the middle and press them together firmly to seal. Crimp the pastry edges with your thumb and forefinger. Remember which end the apple is at!

Brush the top of the pastry with egg wash. For the glaze, mix the sugar and spice together and sprinkle over the apple end of the pastry.

Place the pasties on the lined baking tray and bake in the oven for 10 minutes, then lower the oven setting to 200°C/180°C Fan/Gas 6 and cook for another 15 minutes until golden brown.

Harissa chicken, tomato and olive pasties

It's a sad day when there's not a jar of harissa in my fridge; it's such a versatile seasoning. Here, it really brings the filling ingredients together and when I bake these I love the sight of its bright red oil escaping from any tiny crack in the pastry – it's a sign of promising things to come.

Makes 4 large pasties

750g shortcrust pastry (page 16), made with half butter, half lard
Flour, to dust
Egg wash (beaten egg)

For the filling
4 organic or free-range chicken thighs (bone in)
3 tbsp olive oil
2 medium or 1 large sweet potatoes, peeled and cut into 2cm cubes
100g sun-dried tomatoes
75g kalamata olives, pitted and roughly chopped
A small bunch of dill, leaves picked and finely chopped
1 generous tbsp rose harissa (more if you like it hot!)
Sea salt and freshly cracked black pepper

Preheat the oven to 180°C/160°C Fan/Gas 4.

For the filling, put the chicken thighs into a roasting tray, trickle over 1 tbsp olive oil, season and roast for 1–1½ hours until very tender. Transfer to a plate and set aside.

Turn the oven up to 200°C/180°C Fan/Gas 6. Add the sweet potatoes to the (now empty) roasting tray. Trickle over the remaining 2 tbsp olive oil, season and roast for 15–20 minutes until tender.

Pick the chicken from the bones and chop it, keeping any skin and juices. Finely chop the skin. Put all the chicken and juices into a large bowl with the sweet potatoes and remaining filling ingredients. Mix well, breaking up some of the potatoes to bind the mix. Check the seasoning.

Turn the oven up to 220°C/200°C Fan/Gas 7. Line a baking tray with baking paper. Divide the pastry into 4 portions. Roll each out to a rough circle, 3mm thick, and trim to a 22cm round, using an upturned plate or loose-bottomed cake/flan tin base as a guide.

Pile a quarter of the filling onto one side of each pastry round, leaving a 3cm clear border. Brush this border with egg wash, then fold the other side of the pastry over the filling and bring the edges together. Press the pastry edges firmly to seal and crimp them. Brush the top of the pastry with egg wash.

Lay the pasties on the baking tray and bake for 10 minutes then lower the oven setting to 200°C/180°C Fan/Gas 6 and cook for another 15 minutes until golden brown.

Cheese, onion and roast potato pasties

Ever popular, shop-bought cheese and onion pasties always include some potato, so I decided to come up with my own recipe, hoping to take these pasties to another level. Here I roast the potatoes first so they take on a chip-like flavour, and sweat the onions down with a good hit of thyme to develop a mellow sweetness. This version is the best I've made yet.

Makes 4 large pasties

750g shortcrust pastry (page 16)
Flour, to dust
Egg wash (beaten egg)

For the filling
500g floury potatoes, such as
   Maris Piper or King Edward,
   peeled and cut into 2cm cubes
2 tbsp sunflower oil
2 tbsp extra virgin olive oil
4 medium onions, sliced
4 sprigs of thyme
200g mature Cheddar, grated
Sea salt and freshly cracked
   black pepper

Preheat the oven to 220°C/200°C Fan/Gas 7.

For the filling, put the cubed potatoes on a baking tray. Trickle over the sunflower oil, season with salt and pepper and toss well. Bake in the oven for 20–25 minutes until just cooked. Remove and leave to cool.

Meanwhile, place a saucepan over a medium heat. Add the olive oil, followed by the onions with the thyme, and cook for 7–10 minutes until softened. Remove from the heat and pick out the thyme stalks. Leave to cool slightly.

Tip the cooled potatoes into a large bowl and crush them lightly with the back of a fork. Add the onions and cheese and mix well. Taste and season accordingly.

Line a baking tray with baking paper. Divide the pastry into 4 portions. Roll each out on a lightly floured surface to a rough circle, 3mm thick, and trim to a neat 22cm round, using an upturned plate or loose-bottomed cake/flan tin base as a guide.

Pile a quarter of the filling onto one side of each pastry round, leaving a 3cm margin around the edge. Brush this border with egg wash. Fold the other side of the pastry over the filling and bring the edges together. Press these firmly to seal and crimp them with your thumb and forefinger. Brush the top of the pastry with egg wash.

Lay the pasties on the lined tray and bake for 10 minutes, then lower the oven setting to 200°C/180°C Fan/Gas 6 and cook for another 15 minutes until golden brown.

Ratatouille pasties

I love a ratatouille and this roasted version is made all in one tray in the oven, thereby maximising the flavour, while keeping the washing up down. The pasties smell amazing, but don't be tempted to eat them straight from the oven – the cherry tomatoes stay seriously hot for quite a while!

Makes 4 large pasties

750g shortcrust pastry (page 16)
Flour, to dust
Egg wash (beaten egg)

For the filling
2 medium red onions, cut into
   2cm dice
4 garlic cloves, roughly chopped
1 courgette, cut into 2cm dice
1 aubergine, cut into 2cm dice
4 tbsp extra virgin olive oil
150g cherry tomatoes
100g kalamata olives, pitted
   and roughly chopped
400g tin chopped tomatoes
A bunch of basil, leaves picked
   and torn
Sea salt and freshly cracked
   black pepper

Preheat the oven to 210°C/190°C Fan/Gas 6½.

For the filling, put the onions, garlic, courgette and aubergine into a roasting tray. Trickle over the olive oil, season with salt and pepper and toss well. Cook in the oven for 30 minutes, stirring halfway through.

Add the cherry tomatoes, olives and chopped tomatoes and return to the oven for 20 minutes, stirring halfway through. Remove from the oven and stir through the basil leaves. Taste and adjust the seasoning if necessary then allow to cool.

Turn the oven setting up to 220°C/200°C Fan/Gas 7. Line a baking tray with baking paper. Divide the pastry into 4 portions. Roll each out on a lightly floured surface to a rough circle, 3mm thick, and trim to a neat 22cm round, using an upturned plate or loose-bottomed cake/flan tin base as a guide.

Pile a quarter of the filling mixture onto one side of each pastry round, leaving a 3cm clear margin around the edge. Brush the pastry border with egg wash, then fold the other side of the pastry over the filling and bring the edges together. Press the pastry edges firmly to seal and crimp them with your thumb and forefinger. Brush the top of the pastry with egg wash.

Place the pasties on the lined baking tray and bake in the oven for 10 minutes, then lower the oven setting to 200°C/180°C Fan/Gas 6 and cook for another 15 minutes until golden brown. Serve with a leafy salad on the side.

Curried cauliflower pasties

Cauliflower curry is one of my favourite things to eat and to be able to transport one around in a handy-to-eat pasty is just a dream! Binding the curry with yoghurt makes all the difference to the filling. A regular in our picnic box and my lunch box, this has been a family favourite for a while.

Makes 4 large pasties

750g shortcrust pastry (page 16)
Flour, to dust
Egg wash (beaten egg)

For the filling
300g new potatoes, halved
2 tbsp sunflower oil
1 medium cauliflower
1 onion, finely chopped
1 red pepper, cored, deseeded
   and finely chopped
2 tbsp medium-heat curry powder
1 tsp ground cumin
1 tsp ground coriander
1 tsp nigella seeds
3 tbsp light rapeseed oil
150g natural yoghurt
A small bunch of mint, leaves
   picked and finely chopped
Sea salt and freshly cracked
   black pepper

Preheat the oven to 220°C/200°C Fan/Gas 7. Tip the new potatoes onto a large roasting tray, trickle over the sunflower oil and toss to coat. Roast in the oven for 15–20 minutes until golden, stirring halfway through.

Meanwhile, remove the outer leaves from the cauliflower and finely slice them. Break off the florets from the stem and cut into small pieces; finely dice the stem. Put all the cauliflower into a large bowl with the onion and red pepper. Add the spices and toss to mix.

Remove the tray from the oven and add the cauliflower and onion. Trickle over the rapeseed oil and give it all a good stir. Return to the oven for 12–15 minutes until the veg are soft. Tip into a large bowl and break up the potatoes with the back of a fork. Let cool slightly, then add the yoghurt and mint, mix well and season to taste.

Line a baking tray with baking paper. Divide the pastry into 4 portions. Roll each out to a rough circle, 3mm thick, and trim to a neat 22cm round, using an upturned plate or loose-bottomed cake/flan tin base as a guide.

Pile a quarter of the filling onto one side of each pastry round, leaving a 3cm clear border. Brush this border with egg wash, then fold the other side of the pastry over the filling and bring the edges together. Press them firmly to seal and crimp with your thumb and forefinger. Brush the top of the pastry with egg wash.

Lay the pasties on the lined tray. Bake for 10 minutes, then lower the oven setting to 200°C/180°C Fan/Gas 6 and cook for another 15 minutes until golden brown.

Three bean chilli pasties

The veggie filling for these pasties is really quick to make – a brief sweat of onions, red pepper and spices and you're nearly there. Use whatever beans you fancy but a variety is key, so go for at least three different kinds. These pasties are always a resounding success and a touch more interesting than your standard veg pasty.

Makes 4 large pasties

750g shortcrust pastry (page 16)
Flour, to dust
Egg wash (beaten egg)

For the filling
2 tbsp sunflower oil
2 onions, diced
3 garlic cloves, finely chopped
1 red pepper, cored, deseeded
   and finely chopped
1 medium-heat red chilli, deseeded
   and finely chopped
1 tbsp ground cumin
1 tbsp paprika
750g tinned beans (drained
   weight, about 3 x 400g tins),
   such as kidney beans, black beans
   and cannellini beans, rinsed
1 heaped tbsp tomato purée
A small bunch of coriander, leaves
   picked and roughly chopped
Sea salt and freshly cracked
   black pepper

Place a saucepan over a medium heat and add the sunflower oil followed by the onions, garlic, red pepper and chilli. Cook, stirring often, for 10 minutes or until the onions are softened.

Add the spices and cook for a couple of minutes, stirring constantly to stop them from burning. Add the beans, tomato purée and chopped coriander, stirring so the purée binds the ingredients. Taste and season accordingly. Allow to cool.

Preheat the oven to 220°C/200°C Fan/Gas 7. Line a baking tray with baking paper. Divide the pastry into 4 portions. Roll each out on a lightly floured surface to a rough circle, 3mm thick, and trim to a neat 22cm round, using an upturned plate or loose-bottomed cake/flan tin base as a guide.

Pile a quarter of the filling mixture onto one side of each pastry round, leaving a 3cm clear margin around the edge. Brush the pastry border with egg wash, then fold the other side of the pastry over the filling and bring the edges together. Press the pastry edges firmly to seal and crimp them with your thumb and forefinger. Brush the top of the pastry with egg wash.

Place the pasties on the lined baking tray and bake in the oven for 10 minutes, then lower the oven setting to 200°C/180°C Fan/Gas 6 and cook for another 15 minutes until golden brown.

7
SWEET PIES, TARTS & PASTRIES

Pudding, dessert, sweet, afters – whatever you choose to call it in your house, everyone has their favourite and it will often involve some form of pastry. I don't serve up a proper dessert every day, but at least once a week I'm likely to. Sweet pies and tarts, lovingly prepared at home, are a great choice – always well received and a far cry from shop-bought alternatives.

For a magical end to a Sunday lunch, I'll often serve up a fruit pie or tart showcasing seasonal fruit, whether it's a winter warming Bramley apple pie, like the one on page 190, or my summery Fresh currant and almond lattice tart (page 202) when blackcurrants and redcurrants are ripe for picking.

There are teatime treats too: sumptuous éclairs filled with a cardamom-scented cream and topped with a salted caramel glaze (on page 220) and old-fashioned Eccles cakes with a twist – a lovely filling of tangy dried apricots and crunchy pumpkin seeds (see page 219).

If you just get comfortable and confident with the pastry recipes used through this chapter, you'll be able to make great desserts and fabulous indulgent treats for all kinds of occasion. If you're after a centrepiece for a special celebration, make my Gâteau St Honoré (page 223); it never fails to impress... or satisfy.

River Cottage Bramley apple pie

As I grew up, I loved my mum's apple pie, made with scrumped, sharp cooking apples from a nearby old, abandoned orchard, and crunchy pastry topped with demerara sugar. This recipe is similar, but I sweeten the apples with muscovado instead of caster sugar to give a hint of toffee. Make sure you don't stew the apples completely – you want chunks of apple with a bit of texture to them in your pie. And, of course, custard, cream or ice cream is a must! *(The baked pie is illustrated on pages 12–13)*

Serves 6

750g sweet pastry (page 20)
Flour, to dust
Egg wash (beaten egg)

For the filling
1.5kg Bramley apples
50g unsalted butter
100g dark muscovado sugar
1 cinnamon stick
4 sprigs of thyme

For the glaze
50g demerara sugar
½ tsp ground mixed spice

To serve
Vanilla custard (page 236),
    cream or vanilla ice cream

Preheat the oven to 190°C/170°C Fan/Gas 5.

For the filling, peel, quarter and core the apples then cut into large chunks and tip into a pan. Add the butter, muscovado sugar, cinnamon and thyme and place over a medium-high heat to melt the butter and sugar.

Continue to cook, stirring regularly, for about 10 minutes to soften the apples slightly. Pick out and discard the cinnamon stick and thyme sprigs.

Transfer the apples to a pie dish, about 25cm in diameter and 3cm deep. Leave to cool.

Roll out the pastry on a lightly floured surface to a 1cm thickness. Lift the pastry on the rolling pin and drape it over the apple filling. Press the edges onto the rim of the pie dish and trim away the excess pastry. Crimp the edges and brush the pastry with egg wash.

Mix the demerara sugar and mixed spice together and sprinkle evenly over the pie lid. Pierce the pastry in a couple of places. Place the pie in the oven and bake for 25–30 minutes, until the pastry is golden brown.

Serve the apple pie hot with lashings of custard, or cream or ice cream if you prefer.

Treacle toffee pear strudel

Treacle toffee always reminds me of bonfire night as it's something we'd have as kids while watching the fireworks, and this dessert is perfect to warm you up on a chilly evening. For me, the best bit is the sauce that escapes and becomes brittle and toffee-like on the tray.

Serves 6

750g rough puff pastry (page 28)
Flour, to dust
Egg wash (beaten egg)

For the filling
6 firm pears
50g butter
50g dark muscovado sugar
1 tsp black treacle
75ml double cream
A pinch of sea salt

For the glaze
20g demerara sugar
½ tsp ground mixed spice

To serve
Vanilla custard (page 236),
    cream or vanilla ice cream

Preheat the oven to 200°C/180°C Fan/Gas 6. Line a baking tray with baking paper.

For the filling, halve, peel and core the pears and cut into 2cm cubes. Put the butter, sugar and treacle into a saucepan over a medium heat and heat until melted to form a smooth paste. Add the cream and salt and bring to the boil. Add the pears and cook briefly until they just start to soften, then remove from the heat and allow to cool completely.

Roll out the pastry on a lightly floured surface to a rectangle, roughly 25 x 15cm. Brush the outer 2cm with egg wash. Spoon the cold pear mixture evenly onto the middle of the pastry then fold in the two short sides, followed by the longer sides to enclose the filling. Pinch the pastry edges together firmly to seal and then flip over onto the baking tray.

Mix the demerara sugar and spice together in a small bowl. Brush the strudel with egg wash and immediately sprinkle the spiced sugar over the pastry so it adheres to the egg wash before it dries.

Score the top of the strudel at 2cm intervals, then place in the oven. Bake for 25–30 minutes until golden brown.

Serve hot from the oven with custard, cream or ice cream, bearing in mind the filling will be very hot!

Cherry, port and walnut pie

This is a grown-up version of cherry pie as the cherries are cooked in a lovely port syrup infused with spices. Fresh cherries are wonderful, but when they are out of season I have no problem using frozen ones, and they come ready pitted. I don't put pastry on the bottom, as traditional recipes suggest, because it's almost impossible to stop it going soggy.

Serves 6

500g sweet pastry (page 20)
Flour, to dust
Egg wash (beaten egg)

For the filling
150ml port
150ml full-bodied red wine
150g golden caster sugar
Finely grated zest and juice
  of 1 orange
2 star anise
2 juniper berries, bashed
1kg black cherries, pitted
250g walnut halves

To serve
Vanilla custard (page 236),
  cream or vanilla ice cream

Preheat the oven to 220°C/200°C Fan/Gas 7.

To prepare the filling, put the port, red wine, sugar, orange zest and juice, star anise and juniper berries into a saucepan. Place over a high heat to dissolve the sugar and bring to the boil. Cook steadily until the liquor is reduced to a thick syrup; it should register 110°C on a sugar thermometer. Carefully pick out the juniper and star anise.

Add the cherries and walnuts to the sugar syrup and cook for about 10 minutes until the cherries just soften and you have a lovely thick fruit and nut mixture. Remove from the heat and allow to cool.

Transfer the cooled filling to a pie dish, about 25 x 15cm. For the pie lid, roll out the pastry on a lightly floured surface to a large round, just under 1cm thick. Drape it over the filling and press the edges onto the rim of the pie dish to seal. Trim away the excess pastry and crimp the edges.

Brush the pie lid with egg wash and pierce in a couple of places. Place in the oven and bake for 10 minutes, then lower the oven setting to 200°C/180°C Fan/Gas 6 and cook for a further 25–30 minutes until golden brown.

Serve the cherry pie hot from the oven with custard, cream or ice cream.

Gooseberry, strawberry and mint crumble tart

Gooseberries and strawberries were made to be together. Their seasons collide so we get top-quality specimens for a few weeks, and when paired they lift each other's flavours. Cooking them together only intensifies their flavours further. Don't be tempted to pack the crumble down on top of the fruit, just pile it on loosely. As the pie cooks the fruit drops and the crumble falls into the gaps, which means it won't be all cakey and claggy.

Serves 6

300g sweet pastry (page 20)
Butter, to grease
Flour, to dust
Egg wash (beaten egg)

For the filling
300g gooseberries (fresh or
   frozen and thawed)
50g golden caster sugar
350g strawberries, halved
2 sprigs of mint, leaves picked
   and finely chopped
About 1 tbsp cornflour, mixed to
   a paste with a little cold water

For the crumble
200g plain flour
50g oats
50g sunflower seeds
100g cold butter, diced
50g caster sugar
A pinch of sea salt

To serve
Vanilla ice cream

Preheat the oven to 180°C/160°C Fan/Gas 4. Grease and flour a 20cm tart tin, 4cm deep, and place on a baking sheet.

Roll out the pastry on a lightly floured surface and use to line the tart tin (as described on page 24). Prick the pastry, line with baking paper and baking beans and bake blind, then trim and seal (as detailed on page 27).

For the filling, tip the gooseberries into a shallow roasting tray and sprinkle the sugar evenly over them. Cook in the oven for 8 minutes, then take out the tray and add the strawberries. Gently mix together and allow to cool.

Strain the juice from the fruit into a saucepan (there will be a lot of it); do this carefully so you don't break up the fruit. Bring to a gentle simmer and add the chopped mint. Slowly trickle in the cornflour paste, stirring as you do so, until the sauce thickens (you may not need it all). Remove from the heat and leave to cool for 5 minutes or so, then add the fruit and gently fold through.

To make the crumble, put all of the ingredients into a large bowl and rub together with your fingertips or the palms of your hands until you have a rough sand-textured mixture with some bits of butter still intact.

Spoon the fruit filling into the tart case and sprinkle the crumble over the surface; don't be tempted to pack it. Bake in the oven for 40–50 minutes until the crumble is golden brown and crunchy. Serve hot, with ice cream.

Apple and thyme tarte tatin

This French classic was one of the first desserts I learnt to make in a professional kitchen and my earliest attempts weren't great as I was nervous about burning the caramel. It's really important for the end result to get the caramel to that deep golden-brown colour it reaches just before it burns (around 168°C). I like to leave the skin on the apples but feel free to peel them if you prefer.

Serves 6

300g rough puff pastry (page 28)
Flour, to dust

For the filling
750g crisp dessert apples, such
   as Cox or Braeburn
100g caster sugar
A generous pinch of sea salt
60g unsalted butter, in pieces
4 sprigs of thyme

To serve
Crème fraîche

Preheat the oven to 200°C/180°C Fan/Gas 6.

For the filling, quarter and core the apples.

Place a 25cm cast-iron frying pan over a high heat and add the sugar and salt. Stir occasionally until the sugar is melted and continue to cook for about 5 minutes until the mixture forms a dark brown caramel. This will be extremely hot so be careful.

Add the butter to the caramel and, once it is melted, carefully add the apples with the thyme. Toss until all the fruit is coated in caramel. Put to one side.

Roll out the pastry on a lightly floured surface to a 3mm thickness and cut a round that will generously cover the frying pan.

Using a spoon, carefully position the apples in the pan in a single layer, with the rounded sides sitting on the bottom. Drape the pastry over the apples and carefully tuck in the edges around the inside of the pan. Pierce the pastry in a couple of places, then transfer to the oven. Bake for 25 minutes or until the pastry is golden.

Leave the tatin to stand for 5 minutes, then invert a serving plate over the top of the pan. Holding the pan and plate closely together, flip them both over so the tarte tatin is released onto the plate. Serve hot or cold with crème fraîche.

Vanilla and nutmeg custard tart

Who makes the best custard tart is a hotly debated topic in the chef community, and this is the best recipe I've come to over the years. The keys to success are: avoid overwhisking the mixture and incorporating too much air; skim off all of the foam that rises to the top so you get a beautiful smooth top for the nutmeg to stick to, and keep the oven low so the custard doesn't soufflé on baking.

Serves 6

250g sweet pastry (page 20)
Butter, to grease
Flour, to dust
Egg wash (beaten egg)

For the filling
500ml double cream
1 vanilla pod, split lengthways
   and seeds scraped out
10 medium egg yolks
50g golden caster sugar
1 nutmeg, for grating

To serve (optional)
Fresh berries

Preheat the oven to 180°C/160°C Fan/Gas 4. Grease and flour a 20cm tart tin, 3cm deep, and place on a baking sheet. Roll out the pastry on a lightly floured surface and use to line the tart tin (see page 24). Prick the pastry, line with baking paper and baking beans and bake blind, then trim and seal (as detailed on page 27). Lower the oven setting to 140°C/120°C Fan/Gas 1.

For the filling, pour the cream into a saucepan and add the vanilla pod and seeds. Slowly bring to the boil over a medium-low heat. Meanwhile, whisk the egg yolks and sugar together in a bowl until combined.

Once boiling, pick out the vanilla pod and pour the cream onto the egg mix, whisking as you do so. Stop whisking as soon as it is all added. Leave to stand for 30 minutes to allow any air bubbles to escape, then skim off any froth.

Position a shelf towards the bottom of the oven; take the other shelves out. Pour half of the mixture into the tart case, and place on the shelf in the oven. Once in position, pour in the rest of the custard mixture. (This enables you to fill the case to the brim without spillage.)

Grate the nutmeg liberally over the surface of the custard, then gently close the oven door. Cook for 45–50 minutes until the silky custard is set enough to just stop wobbling in the middle. Remove from the oven and leave to cool.

Serve the tart at room temperature or chilled, with fresh berries on the side if you like.

Fresh currant and almond lattice tart

I love the fresh currant season but it is super-short so we usually freeze some of our crop to enjoy them for longer. You can use either fresh or frozen fruit for this tart. The sharpness of both red- and blackcurrants works magically with the sweet almond filling. As the seasons change, you can vary the fruit – even apples and pears work for a winter dessert.

Serves 12

500g sweet pastry (page 20)
Butter, to grease
Flour, to dust
Egg wash (beaten egg)

For the filling
200g unsalted butter, softened
200g soft light brown sugar
3 medium eggs
200g ground almonds
200g redcurrants (fresh or
  frozen and thawed)
150g blackcurrants (fresh or
  frozen and thawed)

To serve
Crème anglaise (page 238)

Preheat the oven to 180°C/160°C Fan/Gas 4. Grease and flour a 25cm tart tin, 3cm deep, and place on a baking sheet.

Roll out three-quarters (375g) of the pastry on a lightly floured surface and use to line the tin (as described on page 24). Prick the pastry, line with baking paper and baking beans and bake blind, then trim and seal (as detailed on page 27).

For the filling, in a large bowl beat the butter and sugar together thoroughly until creamy. Beat in the eggs, one at a time, until just incorporated then fold in the ground almonds. Gently fold in the red- and blackcurrants and use to fill the tart case.

Roll out the remaining pastry to a rectangle, the same length as the diameter of your tart and about half of the width. Run a lattice roller cutter along the length of the pastry and then carefully stretch the pastry widthways, to open out the lattice.

Brush the pastry edge of the tart case with egg wash and then carefully drape the pastry lattice over the filling. Press the lattice ends onto the edges of the pastry case. Gently brush the pastry lattice with egg wash.

Place in the oven and bake for 40–50 minutes until the almond filling is fully cooked in the middle.

Serve the lattice tart warm or at room temperature with crème anglaise.

Bougatsa

This goes hand in hand with the spanakopita on page 51, a staple order for breakfast in Greece, especially from the youngest member of our family who couldn't quite believe it was ok to have pudding for breakfast! This semolina custard is rich and smooth and sets on baking, so you can easily cut it into generous slices to hand out. You are normally given the option of having cinnamon sugar dusted on the top but for me it's a must.

Serves 8–10

6 filo pastry sheets, about
   350g in total (page 37)
60g butter, melted

For the filling
1 litre whole milk
1 vanilla pod, split lengthways
   and seeds scraped out
4 medium eggs
150g golden caster sugar
100g fine semolina

To finish
50g icing sugar
1 tsp ground cinnamon

Preheat the oven to 210°C/190°C Fan/Gas 6½.

For the filling, pour the milk into a saucepan and add the vanilla pod and seeds. Slowly bring to the boil over a medium-low heat.

Meanwhile, whisk the eggs and sugar together in a large bowl until smoothly combined. Whisk in the semolina, a little at a time. Pick out the vanilla pod from the milk then slowly add to the whisked mixture, whisking all the time. Once combined, pour back into the pan and return to a low heat. Cook, stirring constantly, for about 10 minutes until thickened and smooth. Remove from the heat and allow to cool.

Brush a deep 25cm tart tin or a roasting tin, about 25 x 20cm, with melted butter, then line with 3 sheets of filo pastry, letting the excess overhang the rim of the tin. Spoon in the custard and spread evenly. Fold the overhanging filo over the top and cover with another 3 filo sheets, brushing them with melted butter and scrunching them to fit. Brush with the remaining butter.

Place in the oven and bake for 15 minutes, then lower the oven setting to 180°C/160°C Fan/Gas 4 and cook for a further 20 minutes or until the pastry is golden brown. Remove from the oven and allow to cool slightly.

Mix the icing sugar and cinnamon together in a small bowl. Dust the pie liberally with the cinnamon sugar before cutting into slices to serve.

Marmalade and whisky treacle tart

When I was younger, I had a sweeter tooth and I loved a classic treacle tart with its golden syrup filling. Now that I'm less tolerant to overly sweet things, I much prefer this version. Coming across little strips of citrus rind in the filling is a joy so I like to choose a marmalade that has plenty of rind. You'll also get a lovely warmth from the glug of whisky – it's the perfect tart for a Burns night celebration.

Serves 8

300g shortcrust pastry (page 16)
Butter, to grease
Flour, to dust
Egg wash (beaten egg)

For the filling
500g marmalade
3 medium eggs
150g double cream
100ml whisky
90g soft wholemeal breadcrumbs
60g ground almonds
A pinch of sea salt

To serve
Whipped cream

Preheat the oven to 180°C/160°C Fan/Gas 4. Grease and flour a 20cm tart tin, 4cm deep, and place on a baking sheet.

Roll out the pastry on a lightly floured surface and use to line the tin (as described on page 24). Prick the pastry, line with baking paper and baking beans and bake blind, then trim and seal (as detailed on page 27).

For the filling, melt the marmalade in a pan over a low heat, stirring, then take off the heat.

Whisk the eggs, cream and whisky together in a large bowl, then add the breadcrumbs, ground almonds, salt and most of the marmalade, setting aside 1 tbsp of the liquid (i.e. without rind). Mix thoroughly.

Spoon the mixture into the tart case and spread evenly. Bake for 30–35 minutes until the filling is just set in the middle; you don't want it to rise too much.

Remove from the oven and, while still warm, brush the reserved marmalade over the surface to give the tart a wonderful sheen. Serve with whipped cream.

Plum, raspberry and hazelnut meringue pie

I've always loved meringue pies but here, instead of the classic lemon flavour, I'm using homegrown plums and raspberries. They're perfect partners and around together for a good stint towards the end of summer.

Serves 6–8

300g sweet pastry (page 20)
Butter, to grease
Flour, to dust
Egg wash (beaten egg)

For the fruit
400g plums, halved and stoned
10g butter, in tiny pieces
300g raspberries

For the crème pâtissière
4 egg yolks (whites kept for
   the meringue, below)
60g caster sugar
25g plain flour
2 tsp cornflour
280ml whole milk
100g hazelnuts, toasted
   and bashed
1 vanilla pod, split lengthways
   and seeds scraped out

For the meringue
4 egg whites
140g caster sugar

Preheat the oven to 180°C/160°C Fan/Gas 4. Grease and flour a 22cm tart tin, 3cm deep, and place on a baking sheet. Roll out the pastry on a lightly floured surface and use to line the tin (as described on page 24). Prick the pastry, line with baking paper and baking beans and bake blind, then trim and seal (as detailed on page 27).

Turn the oven up to 200°C/180°C Fan/Gas 6. For the filling, place the plum halves on a roasting tray, cut side up, and pop a little butter into each stone hollow. Bake for 10–20 minutes, depending on ripeness, until you can pierce the fruit easily with a knife. Turn the oven down to 190°C/170°C Fan/Gas 5.

For the crème pâtissière, whisk the egg yolks, sugar, flour and cornflour together in a bowl to combine. Put the milk, nuts, vanilla pod and seeds into a pan and slowly bring to the boil. Pick out the vanilla pod then pour onto the egg mix, whisking as you do so. Return to the pan and bring to the boil, stirring. Simmer, stirring, for 1–2 minutes.

Pour the crème pâtissière into the pastry case and spread evenly. Sit the plum halves in the crème pâtissière and then scatter the raspberries around them.

For the meringue, in a very clean large bowl, using an electric whisk, whisk the egg whites to stiff peaks. Whisk in the sugar, a spoonful at a time, until it is all incorporated and you have a stiff, shiny meringue.

Dollop the meringue over the top of the fruit in the tart case to cover it completely and use the back of a spoon to peak the surface. Place in the oven for 12–15 minutes until the meringue is tinged brown. Serve hot or cold.

Chocolate, hazelnut and blueberry tart

The talented and lovely Gill Meller, who helped me out with the photographs for this book raised an eyebrow over this recipe. 'Chocolate and blueberries, that's a new one on me,' he said, but it only took one bite to convince him that this is a winning combo. Blueberries have a sharp twang, which goes a long way to stop this being too chocolatey (if there is such a thing). They also give the finished tart an almost purple tinge.

Serves 12

300g sweet pastry (page 20)
Butter, to grease
Flour, to dust
Egg wash (beaten egg)

For the filling
400ml double cream
320g good-quality dark chocolate chips (at least 70% cocoa solids)
2 medium eggs
150g hazelnuts, toasted and bashed into rough pieces
A pinch of sea salt
50ml cider brandy (optional)
100g blueberries

To serve (optional)
Crème fraîche

Preheat the oven to 180°C/160°C Fan/Gas 4. Grease and flour a 22cm tart tin, 3cm deep, and place on a baking sheet.

Roll out the pastry on a lightly floured surface and use to line the tin (as described on page 24). Prick the pastry, line with baking paper and baking beans and bake blind, then trim and seal (as detailed on page 27). Lower the oven setting to 170°C/150°C/Gas 3.

To make the filling, put the cream and chocolate into a saucepan over a low heat and warm gently, stirring constantly, until the chocolate is melted and the mixture is smoothly combined. Remove from the heat and leave to cool slightly.

Beat the eggs together lightly in a large bowl until smoothly combined, then pour on the cooled chocolate mixture, whisking constantly. Now fold in the bashed hazelnuts, salt and cider brandy, if using.

Pour the filling into the tart case. Scatter the blueberries evenly over the surface and poke them gently into the chocolate filling. Bake in the oven for 15–20 minutes until the filling is just set in the centre.

Transfer the tart to a wire rack and leave to cool. Serve at room temperature (definitely not chilled!) with a dollop of crème fraîche if you like.

Fig and blackberry frangipane tart

It's a bit of a liberty to call this 'frangipane', which implies almonds, as I've used ground pumpkin seeds instead, but it does give you an idea of the soft, moist texture to expect from the filling. Toasting gives the pumpkin seeds a full nutty flavour, so don't skimp on this stage, and make sure you blend them finely. I'm confident you'll enjoy this version but feel free to swap in ground almonds – the tart will still be fabulous.

Serves 12

300g sweet pastry (page 20)
Butter, to grease
Flour, to dust
Egg wash (beaten egg)

For the filling
250g pumpkin seeds, plus extra
    to sprinkle
250g unsalted butter, softened
250g soft brown sugar
4 medium eggs
50g plain flour
8 figs, halved vertically
150g blackberries (fresh or
    frozen and thawed)

To serve
Crème anglaise (page 238)
    or vanilla ice cream

Preheat the oven to 180°C/160°C Fan/Gas 4. Grease and flour a 22cm tart tin, 3cm deep, and place on a baking sheet.

Roll out the pastry on a lightly floured surface and use to line the tart tin (as described on page 24). Prick the pastry, line with baking paper and baking beans and bake blind, then trim and seal (as detailed on page 27).

Turn the oven up to 200°C/180°C Fan/Gas 6. Scatter the pumpkin seeds on a baking tray and toast in the oven for 6–8 minutes until nicely coloured. Remove from the oven and allow to cool, then tip into a food processor and blitz as finely as possible (but not until clumped together).

Turn the oven down to 180°C/160°C Fan/Gas 4. In a large bowl, beat the butter and sugar together thoroughly until creamy. Beat in the eggs, one at a time, until just combined, then fold in the pumpkin seeds and flour.

Transfer the frangipane filling to the tart case and spread evenly. Arrange the figs on top, some cut side up, some skin side up, and press gently into the frangipane. Scatter the blackberries around the figs and poke them in too. Scatter a handful of pumpkin seeds over the surface.

Bake the tart in the oven for 40–50 minutes until the frangipane is just cooked in the centre.

Serve the tart warm or at room temperature with crème anglaise or ice cream.

Plum, chocolate and orange lattice tart

This is an indulgent, rich dessert packed with fruit that loves to be paired with chocolate and a nice hit of rum and subtle spice. The key is to use flavourful ripe fruit and great chocolate. Applying a lattice of pastry allows you to keep an eye on the delicate filling as it cooks – you want it to just set and not rise much.

Serves 6–8

400g sweet pastry (page 20)
Butter, to grease
Flour, to dust
Egg wash (beaten egg)

For the filling
500ml double cream
2 oranges
3 star anise
A pinch of sea salt
250g good-quality dark chocolate
    chips (70% cocoa solids)
3 medium eggs
50ml rum (optional)
5 Victoria (or similar) plums,
    halved and stoned

To serve
Crème anglaise (page 238) or
    vanilla ice cream

Preheat the oven to 180°C/160°C Fan/Gas 4. Grease and flour a 22cm tart tin, 3cm deep, and place on a baking sheet.

Roll out 300g of the sweet pastry on a lightly floured surface and use to line the tin (as described on page 24). Prick the pastry, line it with baking paper and baking beans and bake blind, then trim and seal (as detailed on page 27).

Turn the oven down to 170°C/150°C Fan/Gas 3.

For the filling, pour the cream into a medium saucepan and grate the zest from the oranges directly into the pan. Add the star anise and salt. Heat gently over a very low heat to infuse the cream with the flavourings for 5 minutes or so, then pass through a sieve into a bowl.

Add the chocolate to the warm infused cream, whisking as you do so, and continue to whisk until the chocolate is melted and smoothly combined.

In another bowl, lightly beat the eggs and then stir in the warm chocolate mixture and the rum, if using. Set aside.

Stand the oranges on a board and cut off all the white pith. Now, holding the oranges over a bowl to catch the juice, cut in between the membranes to release the orange segments; set aside. Squeeze the orange pulp over the bowl to extract the juice, discarding any pips. Whisk this orange juice into the chocolate mixture.

continued overleaf

Distribute the plum halves evenly in the pastry case and scatter the orange segments around them. Carefully pour on the chocolate mixture.

Roll out the remaining pastry to a rectangle, the same length as the diameter of your tart and about half of the width. Run a lattice roller cutter along the length of the pastry and then carefully stretch the pastry widthways, to open out the lattice.

Brush the pastry edge of the tart case with egg wash and then carefully drape the pastry lattice over the filling. Press the lattice ends onto the edge of the pastry case. Gently brush the pastry lattice with egg wash.

Place the tart in the oven and bake for 40–50 minutes until the chocolate filling is just set in the middle.

Transfer to a wire rack and leave to cool. Serve at room temperature with crème anglaise or ice cream.

Eccles cakes with apricots and pumpkin seeds

These sweet little pastries are traditionally served with a bit of crumbly Lancashire cheese, which is the way my grandad (who was from the county) devoured them. Apricots deliver the sweetness in my version, which is a bit of a departure from the sugar-laden Eccles cakes he would have eaten but I think he would have enjoyed these. We get amazing unsulphured sun-dried apricots, which are full of flavour and well worth seeking out.

Makes 12

500g rough puff pastry (page 28)
Flour, to dust
Egg wash (beaten egg)

For the filling
50g pumpkin seeds
200g dried apricots (unsulphured)
50ml cloudy apple juice

For the glaze
25g demerara sugar
½ tsp ground mixed spice

Preheat the oven to 200°C/180°C Fan/Gas 6 and line a baking sheet with baking paper.

For the filling, scatter the pumpkin seeds on another baking sheet and toast in the oven for 6–8 minutes until nicely coloured. Remove from the oven and allow to cool then tip into a food processor. Blitz the seeds for a couple seconds to break them up, then add the apricots and apple juice and blitz to a rough paste.

Roll out the pastry on a lightly floured surface and cut out 12 rounds, 8cm in diameter. Dollop a heaped teaspoonful of the filling in the centre of each round and brush the edges of the pastry with water. Gather the pastry edges up over the filling and bring them to meet over the top. Pinch together to seal and then flip each pastry over so the seam is underneath. Gently press to flatten into discs and place on the lined baking sheet.

Brush the pastries with egg wash and make a couple of slits in the top of each to allow steam to escape during cooking. Mix the demerara sugar with the mixed spice and sprinkle over the top of the pastries. Bake in the oven for 12–15 minutes until golden brown.

Transfer the Eccles cakes to a wire rack to cool and eat warm or at room temperature. Once cooled, they will keep in an airtight tin for 3 days.

Éclairs with cardamom cream and salted caramel glaze

The salted caramel glaze for these éclairs is stunning. The trick is to use it at just the right temperature so, once made, allow it to cool naturally and keep checking how it drops off a spoon. Once it becomes really thick and is just warm, it will set as it hits the éclairs to give the shiniest finish you can imagine. To get a good caramel, it's worth investing in a digital thermometer to ensure you hit the right temperature.

Makes 4

1 quantity of freshly made choux pastry (page 45)

For the caramel glaze
250g golden caster sugar
50ml water
1 tsp sea salt
150ml double cream
50g butter, diced

For the filling
400ml double cream
200ml natural yoghurt
1 tsp ground cardamom

Preheat the oven to 220°C/210°C Fan/Gas 7 and line a large baking sheet with baking paper. Pipe or spoon the freshly prepared choux pastry into four 10–12cm lengths on the baking sheet, leaving plenty of space in between for them to expand on baking.

Bake in the oven for 10 minutes then lower the oven setting to 210°C/200°C Fan/Gas 6½ and keep cooking for a further 10–15 minutes until golden brown and crisp. Don't open the oven door until the cooking process is finished, as your choux éclairs will collapse if you do so.

To make the caramel glaze, put the sugar, water and salt into a heavy-based saucepan and place over a medium-high heat. Heat, without stirring, until the sugar melts and takes on a deep golden-brown colour. If it is colouring in different spots of the pan, shake the pan to swish the sugar syrup around but do not stir or it will crystallise.

Once the syrup registers 160°C on a sugar thermometer, carefully add the cream and stir quickly. Gradually add the butter and bring to the boil, stirring, then remove from the heat. Allow to cool until thickened to a glaze.

To make the filling, whip the cream in a bowl until it forms soft peaks. Add the yoghurt and ground cardamom and whisk again until the mixture stiffens.

Split the éclairs through the middle and fill them with the cardamom cream. Spoon the caramel glaze generously on top of the éclairs and leave to set before serving.

Gâteau St Honoré

When I was working as a young chef I was told to get a copy of *Larousse Gastronomique*, which is *the* encyclopaedia of food, with an emphasis on classic French cuisine. I was transfixed by a picture of a Gâteau St Honoré in the book and persuaded my head pastry chef to put individual ones on the menu. I somewhat regretted this a few weeks and a thousand gâteaux later! The impressive dessert still remains a favourite of mine, although I only make the full-size version these days.

Serves 6

250g sweet pastry (page 20)
Butter, to grease
Flour, to dust
Egg wash (beaten egg)
1 quantity of freshly made choux
    pastry (page 45)

For the filling
4 egg yolks
60g caster sugar
25g plain flour
2 tsp cornflour
280ml whole milk
1 vanilla pod, split lengthways
    and seeds scraped out
250ml double cream
Finely grated zest of 1 orange
100ml cider brandy (optional)

For the caramel
150g caster sugar

To finish
100g raspberries
200g mixed soft fruits (halved
    strawberries, blueberries,
    redcurrants etc)

Preheat the oven to 230°C/210°C Fan/Gas 8. Lightly grease two baking trays and line with baking paper.

Roll out the sweet pastry on a lightly floured surface to a 20cm round, no thicker than 3mm (use the removable base of a 20cm tart tin as a guide to cut around).

Place the pastry round on one of the lined trays and pierce all over with a fork. Brush the edge of the pastry round with egg wash.

Put the freshly prepared choux pastry into a piping bag fitted with a 1cm plain nozzle and pipe a ring on the edge of the sweet pastry round, leaving a 5mm clear border on the outside, using about a third of the choux.

Pipe the remaining choux pastry into blobs, the diameter of a 10p piece, on the other lined baking tray.

Place both trays in the oven and bake for 10 minutes then lower the oven setting to 220°C/200°C Fan/Gas 7 and cook for a further 10 minutes or until the choux pastry is golden brown and crisp; don't open the oven during cooking or the choux buns will collapse.

While the pastry is baking, make the crème pâtissière for the filling. Whisk the egg yolks, sugar, flour and cornflour together in a bowl to combine. Put the milk, vanilla pod and seeds into a pan and slowly bring to the boil.

continued overleaf

Pick out the vanilla pod then pour the milk over the egg mix, whisking as you do so. Return the mixture to the pan and bring to the boil, stirring constantly. Simmer, stirring, for 1–2 minutes until thickened and smooth.

Pour the crème pâtissière into a bowl and lay a piece of baking paper directly on the surface to stop a skin forming. Place in the fridge to cool.

When the choux buns and choux-topped pastry round are cooked, transfer them to a wire rack. Pierce the bottom of each of the choux buns. Leave to cool.

Once the crème pâtissière is cooled, whip the cream in a large bowl until it starts to thicken. Add the crème pât, orange zest and brandy, if using, and whisk until thick and smooth. Put some of the cream mixture into the piping bag and pipe into each bun to fill it.

To make the caramel, put the sugar into a heavy-based saucepan with 2 tbsp water and heat, without stirring, until the sugar melts and turns golden, forming a light caramel. If it is colouring in different spots of the pan, shake the pan to swish the sugar syrup around but don't stir or it will crystallise. Take care, as it will be very hot.

Dip the top of each choux bun into the caramel to coat and place on top of the choux pastry ring. Angle each bun so a little caramel runs onto the choux underneath so they stick, and sit the buns snugly next to each other. Drizzle any leftover caramel over the choux border.

Spoon the remaining cream mixture onto the pastry base within the choux border. Put the raspberries into a bowl and crush with a fork. Toss the mixed berries in the raspberry mush and pile into the centre of the gâteau on top of the cream filling. Serve at once, with any remaining berries on the side.

8
GRAVIES, SAUCES & CUSTARD

I love a good slug of extra gravy on pastry and I know I'm not alone, so here is a selection of sauces to finish your savoury pies, plus a couple of custard options for sweet pies and tarts. There's nothing worse than not having enough sauce with pastry, so be sure to make plenty!

Gravy will probably be your go-to sauce for meat pies, so I've given you my recipe on page 230, plus a great beef stock (on page 228), which I guarantee will take your gravy to the next level. Use it for roast dinners as well as the pies in this book. And if you've never tasted London's classic pie liquor, traditionally made with jelly from jellied eels (see page 233), give it a try – it was a game changer for me when I first tasted it. If eel jelly is a step too far, a good fish or chicken stock will do!

So, don't just stop with the pie. Do it justice and make our own gravy to ladle over generously, or creamy, silky custard to finish a sweet pie, strudel or tart. You'll see how that little extra effort makes all the difference.

Beef stock for gravy

Making a good stock is essential for a fine gravy and we are a nation of gravy lovers. For pies and other things that don't create their own gravy in the way a roast does, it is an essential skill. Try to get a pig's trotter in there, as the gelatine and collagen it releases into the sauce help to thicken the stock and lend shine if you're making jus.

Makes 3–4 litres

3kg beef bones, cut into
  5cm pieces
1 pig's trotter
2 onions, halved
2 carrots, roughly chopped
3 celery sticks
1 garlic bulb, halved across
  (through the equator)
3 sprigs of thyme
4 bay leaves
A small bunch of parsley,
  stalks only
2 tsp black peppercorns

Preheat the oven to 230°C/220°C Fan/Gas 8.

Put the beef bones and pig's trotter into a large shallow roasting tray and roast for 20–30 minutes until they have taken on a dark golden brown colour. Remove from the oven and use tongs to transfer the bones to a very large stock pan, leaving the fat behind in the tray. (Pour this fat into a bowl and save for roasting potatoes.)

Now put the veg and garlic into the roasting tray and cook in the oven for 15–20 minutes, giving them a stir halfway through. Add the veg to the bones in the stock pan.

Place the roasting tray over a low heat, add a cup of water and use a spatula to scrape up any residue from the tray. Add this to the stock pan with the thyme, bay leaves, parsley stalks and peppercorns. Pour on enough cold water to cover and gently bring to a simmer.

Turn the heat right down so it's just under a simmer and cook for 24 hours, ideally. If you cannot maintain a very low heat on the hob (or the idea of a pan on overnight is a bit scary!), this can be done in a low oven at 120°C/100°C Fan/Gas ½ – in one or two large deep roasting trays covered in foil. Every so often use a ladle to skim any fat off that has risen to the top. Make sure the liquid is kept topped up and never boils vigorously.

Scoop out the bones and as much of the veg as you possibly can, then pass the liquor through a sieve lined with a thin clean cloth or muslin. This may take a bit of time but it's worth it. You now have stock ready to use.

Gravy

Proper gravy is different from 'jus', as it is typically thickened with flour, which makes it much thicker and more viscous. We use a few extra things here to enhance the flavour, most notably coffee, but just a splash – you don't want your gravy to taste of coffee! If you do happen to have any meat juices knocking around, definitely add them in.

Makes about 1 litre

1.5 litres beef stock (page 228)
200ml full-bodied red wine
100g butter
100g plain flour
2 tbsp tamari or soy sauce
1 tbsp miso
1 tbsp espresso-strength coffee

Pour the beef stock and wine into a saucepan and bring to the boil over a high heat. Boil vigorously until reduced by about one-third.

Melt the butter in a saucepan over a medium-high heat and continue to cook until the butter starts to brown. Add the flour and turn the heat up a bit. Cook, stirring constantly, until the roux (flour mix) starts to brown, but be careful not to burn it!

Start adding the reduced stock, little by little, stirring constantly to avoid lumps forming. Once all the stock is incorporated, add the tamari or soy, miso and coffee.

Simmer for a few minutes until the gravy has lost its floury taste and is lovely and thick. Taste and season appropriately and you're ready to go.

Jus

This word has appeared on many a menu over the last twenty years but what is actually put in front of you is rarely the real deal. An authentic jus is simply a mix of well-reduced good beef stock and reduced red wine. If the stock is good enough you won't even need to add salt. You do need a good homemade stock for this – one that contains gelatine (provided by the pig's trotter) for shine and no salt; bought stock invariably has added salt and is inedibly salty once reduced down.

Makes about 750–900ml

2 litres homemade beef stock
  (page 228)
250ml full-bodied red wine
1 tbsp cider vinegar (optional)
Sea salt (if needed)

Pour the beef stock into a large pan and bring to the boil. Boil rapidly until reduced by at least half. If you've used my recipe on page 228 with a pig's trotter in, it should start to thicken and become glossy.

Put the wine into another saucepan and bring to the boil over a high heat. Let it bubble to reduce right down (until almost completely evaporated), then pour in the reduced stock and stir well.

Now taste the jus. If it seems a bit fatty, add the cider vinegar to counteract this. Season with a little salt if you think it is required, but if the stock you've used is really good you may not need to.

Pie liquor

Although the most common thing for most of us to pour over our pies is gravy, if you're from London you may be more familiar with 'pie liquor'. Before I first tried it, the idea seemed alien, especially when you look back to its historical composition. It stems from a time when jellied or stewed eels were a common, affordable working man's lunch (eels were the only thing that could survive in the polluted Thames). The liquor from the cooking process, which then cools to form the jelly around the eels, was thickened and finished with garlic and parsley to make 'pie liquor'. With the decline of the jellied eel and to suit our modern palate, fish or chicken stock is now more commonly used. This pie liquor is fantastic, so do give it a go. It will transport you back to Victorian London (in a good way) and give you a delicious sauce to enjoy with the mash as well as your pie.

Makes 500ml

50g butter
2 garlic cloves, finely chopped
50g plain flour
500ml chicken or fish stock
   (or jellied eel liquor if you
   can get it!)
A generous bunch of flat-leaf
   parsley, leaves picked and
   finely chopped
Sea salt and freshly cracked
   black pepper

Melt the butter in a saucepan over a low heat, add the garlic and cook for about 5 minutes until it softens. Stir in the flour and cook, stirring, for a couple of minutes, then slowly add the stock, stirring continuously to keep the mixture smooth.

Once the stock is all incorporated, add the chopped parsley and cook, stirring, for a few minutes until the sauce is thickened and has lost its floury taste. Taste and season appropriately.

Béchamel

This is the base for various sauces that go well with lots of the pies in this book, especially the veggie ones. Once you have your béchamel made you can flavour it as you like, adding anything from cheese and mustard to mushrooms (see suggestions below). The world is your oyster!

Makes 500ml

500ml whole milk
8 cloves
4 bay leaves
1 small onion, peeled
50g butter
50g plain flour
Sea salt and freshly ground pepper

Pour the milk into a saucepan. Use the cloves to pin the bay leaves to the onion and pop it into the milk; this is called an onion cloute and is the traditional way to flavour the milk for a béchamel. If you're in a bit of a rush just quarter the onion and add to the milk with the bay leaves and cloves.

Heat the milk really gently over a very low heat – to allow time for the flavours to infuse. Once infused, remove the cloute or strain out the onion, bay leaves and cloves.

Melt the butter in a saucepan over a medium heat. Add the flour and cook, stirring, for a minute or two (without colouring) then slowly add the milk, a little at a time, stirring continuously to avoid lumps forming.

Once the milk is fully incorporated, simmer, stirring, for a few minutes then taste and season accordingly.

Flavouring your béchamel
Whisk in mustard and grated mature Cheddar to taste for a traditional cheese sauce, which goes well with the meatball pie on page 118.

Or add lots of sautéed chopped mushrooms to make a mushroom sauce that's lovely with the cauliflower cheese pie on page 65.

Or simply add an array of chopped herbs to make a fresh-tasting sauce, which will balance the spices in the Merguez spiced squash and apricot pie on page 68.

Velouté

This is a richer version of the béchamel opposite, but one that can be geared to the type of dish it is going to accompany, by using the appropriate stock. The generous glug of cream added at the end gives it a velvety texture, hence the name, velouté (which is French for velvety).

Makes 500ml

30g butter
30g plain flour
300ml chicken, fish or veg stock
200ml double cream
Sea salt and white pepper

Melt the butter in a saucepan over a medium heat. Add the flour and cook, stirring, for a minute or two (without colouring) then slowly add the stock, a little at a time, stirring continuously to avoid lumps forming.

Once the stock is fully incorporated, stir in the cream and simmer, stirring, for a few minutes. Taste and season accordingly.

Flavouring your velouté

Add chopped dill and tarragon to taste for a lovely sauce to accompany the tomato and beetroot steamed pudding on page 56.

Or whisk in some wholegrain mustard and chopped chives to make a delicious creamy sauce to serve with Melle's homity pie on page 88.

Or, for something a little different, add finely chopped preserved lemon (peel only), capers and chopped coriander to taste. This sauce is perfect with the Moroccan lamb shank pie on page 121.

Vanilla custard

A good custard is something to behold and this recipe gives you a rich and creamy custard, without the addition of any thickener. It's a simple method and the chances of it curdling are low. As long as the cream is boiling when you pour it over the egg yolks, the custard thickens without going back on the hob. It's an absolute must for me with the apple pie on page 190 and the pear strudel on page 192.

Makes 500ml

250ml double cream
250ml whole milk
75g golden caster sugar
1 vanilla pod, split lengthways
    and seeds scraped out, or
    2 tsp vanilla extract
4 egg yolks

Put the cream, milk and sugar into a saucepan, add the vanilla pod and seeds, if using, and slowly bring to the boil over a medium heat, stirring occasionally to help dissolve the sugar.

Meanwhile, in a bowl, whisk the egg yolks, together with the vanilla extract, if using. Once the creamy mixture is boiling, take out the vanilla pod if used then slowly pour it onto the egg mixture, whisking as you do so. Swap the whisk for a wooden spoon and stir constantly for a couple of minutes.

By now the mixture will have thickened just enough (for me), but if you want a thicker custard, return it to the saucepan and whisk over a low heat until it reaches the desired consistency.

Pour the custard into a warmed jug to serve.

Note To make a cardamom custard that is particularly good with apple pie, replace the vanilla with 1 tsp ground cardamom, adding it with the sugar.

Crème anglaise

This deliciously rich sauce is served chilled. It is similar to custard, but uses almost all double cream (rather than half cream/half milk). Serve it with any cold, fruity dessert, such as the fresh currant tart on page 202 or the fig and blackberry tart on page 212. Quite frankly, I'm happy just eating it straight out of the bowl.

Makes 600ml

400ml double cream
100ml whole milk
75g golden caster sugar
1 vanilla pod, split lengthways
  and seeds scraped out
4 egg yolks

Put the cream, milk and sugar into a saucepan, add the vanilla pod and seeds and slowly bring to the boil over a medium heat, stirring occasionally to help dissolve the sugar.

Meanwhile, whisk the egg yolks together in a bowl. Once the creamy mixture is boiling, take out the vanilla pod then slowly pour it onto the egg mixture, whisking as you do so.

Swap the whisk for a wooden spoon and stir continuously for a couple of minutes. By now, the mixture should have thickened to make a thin crème anglaise.

Pour the sauce into a jug and cover the surface closely with a disc of baking paper to stop a skin forming, then refrigerate. Serve chilled.

Note The vanilla pod can be rinsed and dried then submerged in a jar of sugar to flavour it.

Directory

We have such amazing farmers, growers and producers in the UK that we should all do our best to support them. Buying SLOW – seasonal, local, organic and wild – is one of our core values at River Cottage, so we'd love to share with you some of our favourite suppliers. Some of these are local to the farm, but I've included great options that are available nationwide, too.

Veg

Our neighbours, Ash and Kate, at the truly brilliant Trill farm, supply organic veg boxes, delivering around Axminster and Lyme Regis. **www.trillfarmgarden.co.uk**

Riverford Organic Farmers have been trailblazers for organic growing since 1986. They deliver organic veg boxes nationwide. **www.riverford.co.uk**

Abel & Cole offer a great selection of organic fruit and veg delivered to your door, as well as many more wonderful organic essentials. **www.abelandcole.co.uk**

Meat

Harry and Emily run a fantastic regenerative, organic farm just 2 miles as the crow flies from River Cottage. Haye Farm supplies organic meat and lots of other organic goodies, with deliveries nationwide. **www.hayefarmdevon.co.uk**

Coombe Farm Organic offers a range of superb organic meats, specialising in retired dairy beef, which is well worth a try. **www.coombefarmorganic.co.uk**

Fish

Based at our local farm shop (Millers), Lyme Bay Fish Shack, run by Nigel and Corinne, offers a great array of fish caught with rod and line or static net from their own boat, as well as other boats landing in Lyme Regis. A must visit if you are in the area. Collection only. **www.millersfarmshop.co.uk**

Lyme Bay Seafood company is a hidden gem, situated in Colyton not far from Lyme Regis, sourcing fish from local boats fishing out of Axmouth and Lyme Regis. Well worth a visit if you're in the locality. Collection only. **www.lymebayseafood.co.uk**

Pesky Fish is an amazing online fishmonger, with a keen eye on sustainability, connecting the fishermen directly with the consumer. They have a daily market to buy from and the fish is delivered to your door in recyclable packaging. **www.peskyfish.co.uk**

Pulses and grains

Hodmedods supply all our pulses and grains – everything from lentils to quinoa – all farmed in the UK and delivered nationwide. **www.hodmedods.co.uk**

Oils

Shipped by Sail import some amazing olive oil from Portugal and it's all shipped here under sail power! You can't get olive oil with a better flavour – and story – anywhere.
www.shippedbysail.org

Organic Yorkshire rapeseed oil, produced by Mike Stringer, is a real treat. You can get it from Hodmedods while shopping for your pulses.
www.hodmedods.co.uk

Dairy

Riverford Organics supply outstanding dairy products as well as vegetables.
www.riverford.co.uk

Milk & More supply dairy products including milk in glass bottles delivered to your door just like milkmen did! They also stock lots of other essentials. Try to pick from their organic range.
www.milkandmore.co.uk

General organic food suppliers

Planet organic is a great one-stop organic shop for all your staples.
www.planetorganic.com

Whole Foods Online is another excellent organic supplier, perfect for topping up your storecupboard.
www.buywholefoodsonline.co.uk

Cookware

Netherton foundry, a fantastic family-run enterprise based in South Shropshire, makes the most fabulous cookware. Examples of their lovely iron work appear through this book, so if you fancy something slightly different to make your pies in, these are your guys!
www.netherton-foundry.co.uk

Index

Acknowledgements

I would never pretend that this book was all down to me and would never want to, so if you're reading this, you'll find out a little about the truly inspirational and exciting people I'm fortunate to spend time with.

My family, Hayley and Willow, are always first and foremost – they are simply the reason for everything. Their love and support has carried me through so much and I'm not sure I'll ever be able to thank and love them enough. Also, thanks to Mitten, Treacle and Lillie for making all our lives so much fun.

Hugh Fearnley-Whittingstall, without you River Cottage simply wouldn't exist. You provide inspiration not only for me but for millions of people around the world. You gave me the belief that together we can all do better, and we can still save this precious earth we are privileged to stand on.

Gill Meller deserves a special shout-out for this book. He helped bring it to life with his amazing ability to make the ordinary extraordinary. I love every minute we get to spend cooking together... long may it continue.

Emma Lee and her assistant Indy are not only great fun to work with but are simply the best at what they do. So, a massive thank you for making this book look so wonderful. I can't wait for the next one... and maybe that podcast.

Janet Illsley, you've been amazing on my last two books, but with this one you have gone above and beyond. I hope you know how much I appreciate it, and you also know how good you really are! And an extra special mention for Will Webb for designing this book and bringing it together in such a fantastic way.

To Rowan Yapp, Emily North, Isobel Turton and the rest of the team at Bloomsbury, thank you for your encouragement and support through all the many stages from initial concept to the final printed book.

To the RC crew, past and present. Over many years I've worked with some of the most fantastic people and a bit of each of you is lodged somewhere in my heart. Special thanks to this bunch of rogues: Connor Reed, Andy Tyrell, Joel Gosling, Sam Lomas, Mark McCabe, Chiara Tomasoni, Jack Botha, Sam Smith, Daniel Harding, Luther Batten, Rachel De Thample, Jonny Callis and Sarah Little.

Bob, you know who you are and what you mean to me and everyone at River Cottage. Stewart Dodd, thank you for your support and faith in me. We're still on this journey together and long may it continue. Here's to the next adventure with plenty of wine!

To the Aldersons: Mum, Dad, Jesse, Amelle and Jon, I hope you love the pies as much as I love you all. Here's to seeing each other a bit more every year!

River Cottage: Food to Inspire Change

From the moment River Cottage came to our TV screens, Hugh has championed a more holistic and sustainable approach to food. He wants us to know where our food comes from, and to understand the consequences of our food choices. For almost three decades now, River Cottage and Hugh have been showing us thatfood can inspire change – both in our lives and in the world around us.

Hugh Fearnley-Whittingstall and his partners at Keo Films created the original River Cottage television series in 1999. The shows ran on Channel 4 in the UK for the next 15 years. The series charted Hugh's culinary adventures, first as a downsizing smallholder at the original River Cottage in West Dorset, and later as he established his cookery school and events venue at the more expansive Park Farm.

River Cottage HQ is now a 90-acre property in an Area of Outstanding Natural Beauty on the Devon/Dorset border. The site was developed and designed under the guidance of architect and sustainability specialist Stewart Dodd, now Chief Executive at River Cottage. Gelf Alderson has been Hugh's chief collaborator since 2012. Hugh, Gelf and their team of chef-tutors now welcome guests from all over the world, teaching them not only how to improve their cooking techniques and artisan food skills, but also how to grow their own ingredients and source food in an ethical and sustainable way.

River Cottage HQ has won many awards, including 'Best Cookery School' in the Great British Food Awards, for three consecutive years. The River Cottage Online Cooking Diploma was launched in 2020 and the Next Level Diploma the following year.

Guests can also stay at Park Farm's beautifully restored seventeenth-century farmhouse and feast on seasonal, local, organic and wild food at regular events in the threshing barn. The River Cottage Kitchen and Store, a restaurant sourcing ingredients from Park Farm and neighbouring organic growers, opened on the site in the spring of 2022.

Hugh and River Cottage have published more than 30 books, including the popular River Cottage Handbook series of practical manuals on artisan cooking techniques, gardening, smallholding and foraging. These books have sold over 2 million copies and won multiple awards, including the Glenfiddich Award, Guild of Food Writers Award, the André Simon Award and, in the US, the James Beard Award.

River Cottage also produces a range of ethically sourced organic products, including yoghurt, kombucha, kefir, sauerkrauts, stocks, sauces, wines, beers and ciders.

BLOOMSBURY PUBLISHING
Bloomsbury Publishing Plc
50 Bedford Square, London, WC1B 3DP, UK
29 Earlsfort Terrace, Dublin 2, Ireland

BLOOMSBURY, BLOOMSBURY PUBLISHING and the Diana logo are
trademarks of Bloomsbury Publishing Plc

First published in Great Britain 2024

A catalogue record for this book is available from the British Library

Library of Congress Cataloguing-in-Publication data has been applied for

ISBN: HB: 9781526639172; ePUB: 9781526639189; ePDF: 9781526639196

10 9 8 7 6 5 4 3 2 1

Project Editor: Janet Illsley
Designer: Will Webb
Photographer: Emma Lee
Food Stylists: Gelf Alderson and Gill Mellor
Indexer: Hilary Bird

Printed and bound by RR Donnelley Ltd, China